Frommer's®

24
GREAT
walks in
AMSTERDAM

D0905298

WILEY

Wiley Publishing, Inc.

Author: Robin Gauldie
Series Editor: Donna Wood
Art Editor: Alison Fenton
Copy Editor: Sharon Amos
Proofreader: Sandy Draper
Picture Researcher: Sarah Hopper
Cartography provided by the Mapping Services
Department of AA Publishing
Image retouching and internal repro: Michael Moody
Production: Stephanie Allen

Edited, designed and produced by AA Publishing.

Published by AA Publishing.

Published in the United States by
Wiley Publishing, Inc.
111 River Street, Hoboken, NJ 07030

Find us online at Frommers.com

Frommer's is a registered trademark of Arthur Frommer.
Used under license.

Mapping © MAIRDUMONT/Falk Verlag 2008

Cartographic Data © Tele Atlas N.V. 2008 **Tele Atlas**

A03625

ISBN 978-0-4704-5368-1

A CIP catalogue record for this book is available from
the British Library.

Colour reproduction by Keene Group, Andover
Printed in China by Leo Paper Group

OPPOSITE: HERENGRACHT CANAL

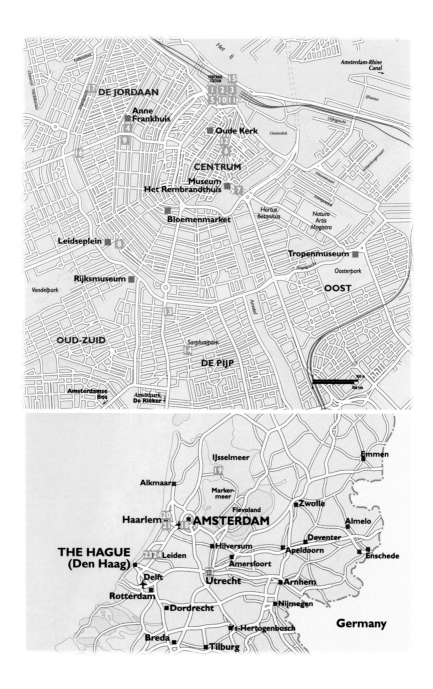

Amsterdam (top map)

Het IJ

Amsterdam-Rhine Canal

CENTRAAL STATION

DE JORDAAN

Anne Frankhuis

Oude Kerk

CENTRUM

Museum Het Rembrandthuis

Bloemenmarket

Hortus Botanicus

Natura Artis Magistra

Leidseplein

Tropenmuseum

Rijksmuseum

Vondelpark

Oosterpark

OOST

OUD-ZUID

Sarphatipark

DE PIJP

Amsterdamse Bos

Amstelpark De Rieker

500 m
500 yds

Netherlands (bottom map)

IJsselmeer

Emmen

Alkmaar

Markermeer

Zwolle

Flevoland

Haarlem

Almelo

AMSTERDAM

Deventer

Apeldoorn

Enschede

THE HAGUE (Den Haag)

Leiden

Hilversum

Amersfoort

Delft

Utrecht

Arnhem

Rotterdam

Nijmegen

Dordrecht

Germany

's-Hertogenbosch

Breda

Tilburg

CONTENTS

Introduction

Amsterdam seems to have been designed with the walker in mind. It is pedestrian friendly, with light traffic and not a hill in sight. The historic centre is compact (you can walk across it in less than an hour), but crammed with sights, museums, and interesting nooks and corners.

Finding your way around is easy, and there are plenty of atmospheric cafés and bars to provide respite for weary feet or shelter from a sudden shower. And walking really helps you see the real city – in all its many guises – beneath the veneer of tourism.

Compared with Rome, Athens, London or Paris, Amsterdam is relatively modern. True, people have lived here for more than a thousand years, but until the 13th century it was no more than a fishing village at the confluence of the Ij and Amstel rivers. Along Amsterdam's rings of canals you won't see many buildings that pre-date the Golden Age of the 17th century. But you will see a unique, architectural heritage, monument to the ingenuity and the perseverance of Amsterdammers down the centuries.

In this book you'll find 24 walks that together capture the essence of Amsterdam, from its earliest history to the present day. You'll see some of the world's most famous works of art, by Rembrandt and his contemporaries, Vincent van Gogh and Andy Warhol (Walk 8) – but you'll also find work by less well-known painters and sculptors. Some of these strolls take you up the steeples of the city's grand landmark churches; others delve into hidden cloisters, courtyards and secret hideaways (Walk 3). Others expose the city's seamier side, from the 'coffee shops' of the Oude Zijd to the notorious red-light district (Walk 11).

Space is precious in Amsterdam, and at first sight it seems to be an intensely built-up city. But some of our walks reveal hidden patches of greenery, or offer you an escape to some of the leafy parks and gardens just beyond the old centre. You'll stroll along the winding paths of the pretty Vondelpark (Walk 8), find botanical evidence of Amsterdam's links with the east in the herb gardens of the Hortus Botanicus (Walk 9), and discover countryside in the city in the Amsterdamse Bos (Walk 18). All the walks in this book are rewarding, but if time is short, Walk 1, Walk 2 and Walk 4 are indispensable

itineraries that help you to discover the best the city has to offer.

Much of what you will see celebrates Amsterdam's long history of pragmatic tolerance – a tradition that continues to this day. But some of these walks recall darker moments, bearing witness to times of intolerance, oppression, and even genocide.

Amsterdam is the kernel of a larger conurbation of smaller towns, often collectively known as the Randstadt. Many of these are virtually suburbs of Amsterdam, and they too have secrets to discover, from ancient universities and churches to streets and buildings that look very much as they appear in the paintings of Frans Hals, Rembrandt and their contemporaries. This book also includes a handful of walks in Utrecht, Haarlem, Leiden and Edam (Walks 19-24).

As you walk, always try to look up and around you. Many of the older buildings retain architectural details such as carved stone gable ornaments, steeped in history. And marvel at the energy and creativity of a city that despite its compact size lives up to its towering reputation.

WHERE TO EAT

€	=	Inexpensive
€€	=	Moderate
€€€	=	Expensive

ABOVE: LEIDEN WINDMILL AT SUNSET

Sampling the City – Around the Dam

The Dam is literally where it all started, and for many visitors – and Amsterdammers – it is still the epicentre of the city.

This walk is designed to give newcomers a first taste of the city, from the grand façade and bustle of Amsterdam Centraal Station to the somewhat quieter backwaters that lie just off the city centre's main thoroughfares. On the way you'll cross the first of many canals. You'll see hints of the city's seamier side, including shop windows crammed with saucy postcards and sex toys, and a much-touted museum of erotica, and you'll probably smell your first whiff of marijuana. You will almost certainly have your first brush with the city's trams and cyclists – both move quietly, and you may not notice their approach until a loud bell announces they are almost upon you. This walk, in short, contains a little of everything that makes Amsterdam so special.

1 Leave Centraal Station by its main entrance. Cross Stationsplein and follow Damrak over the wide bridge that crosses the Open Haven. Continue over the bridge, cross Prins Hendrikkade, and continue down the Damrak to Damrak 28-30.

Damrak is a little tacky, a little sleazy (the Sex Museum at No. 18 is featured in Walk 11), and very commercial, with lots of touristy cafes and souvenir shops interspersed with tall old houses that are typical of the city – so in many ways it's the perfect introduction to the city. Confusingly, the long stretch of water that parallels the street on the opposite side is also called the Damrak. It was once a busy barge harbour, and is still home to a bustling fleet of canal tour boats.

At Damrak 28-30, stop and look up. The frontage of this Jugendstil (Art Nouveau) building was designed by the sculptor J Mendes da Costa (1863-1939), and was inspired by his visits to the Artis Zoo, near his home. Four baboons and 22 owls (count them if you can) look gravely down at you. These are symbols of wisdom that crop up frequently in Mendes da Costa's decorative sculpture on buildings around the Netherlands. Born into Amsterdam's Portuguese-Jewish community, he learned his early skills from his father, a monumental mason, before becoming a leading figure in the Dutch Art Nouveau movement.

2 Cross to the other side of Damrak (next to the water). Turn right, continue walking across Oudebrugsteeg,

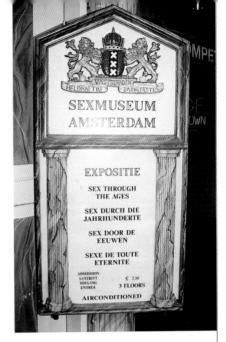

then continue walking further along Damrak to the Beursplein.

The imposing brick pile at Beursplein 1, the Beurs van Berlage, was built in 1903 as Amsterdam's commodities exchange and designed by Hendrick Petrus Berlage. It's strikingly modernistic, with curving lines and an almost unadorned façade. Two slogans on its bell-tower, *Beidt uw Tijd* (Bide your Time) and *Duur uw Uur* (Await your Hour) might have been aimed at the traders within the Beurs – but Berlage was a socialist, so they may have had a more ironic meaning, aimed at the workers outside.

The Beurs van Berlage is now a concert hall (home of the Netherlands Chamber Orchestra and the Netherlands Philharmonic). Occupying the entire east side of Beursplein is the Effectenbeurs,

DISTANCE 1 mile (1.6km)

ALLOW 2.5 hours (add 1.5 hours for full tour of the Historisch Museum)

START Stationsplein in front of Centraal Station

FINISH Spui

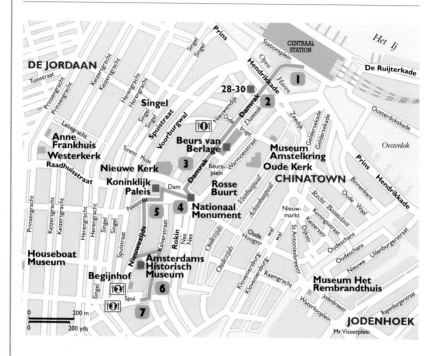

which took over the Beursplein's former role. This Neoclassical building, designed in 1913 by J Th J Cuypers, is a gaudier temple of commerce, with four colossal stone elephant heads supporting its second-floor balcony, and a brightly coloured brick frieze surmounting its upper floor.

3 Face about, go back to Damrak and continue down one block to the Dam, Amsterdam's main square. Damrak and its extension, Rokin, cut the square

in two halves. Turn left and cross the eastern section diagonally to the Nationaal Monument.

In the early 12th century, the local lord, Gijsbrecht I van Amstel, built a castle here. There's nothing left of it, but under his successors, between 1204 and 1275, the River Amstel was dammed and the village that grew up became known as Aemstelle Dam – the dam on the Amstel. The Nationaal Monument dominates the east half of the square. This monolithic

72ft (22m) monument to the Dutch victims of World War II was sculpted by JW Radeler and erected on 4 May 1956, the 11th anniversary of the liberation of the city of Amsterdam.

4 Turn your back on the Nationaal Monument and you'll see the Koninklijk Paleis (Royal Palace) dominating the whole west end of the Dam, less than 100yd (91m) away. Cross Damrak/Rokin and walk across the square to the entrance.

Europe is littered with grand royal buildings that are now the presidential palaces of modern republics; this Baroque-Classical pile was designed by Jacob van Campen (1595-1657) and built between 1648 and 1655 – the apogee of the Golden Age of the Dutch Republic – as Amsterdam's Town Hall. It didn't become a royal palace until 1808, when Napoleon Bonaparte installed his brother Louis as King of the Dutch – and the Bonapartes, of course, both started life as republicans. It has been the Amsterdam home of the kings and queens of the House of Orange ever since Louis fled in 1814. The current monarch, Queen Beatrix, divides her time between her Amsterdam residence and a second palace in the Hague. Inside, you can't miss the huge 91ft (28m) Burgerzaal (Citizens' Hall). Lined in marble, it has a magnificent floor inlaid with maps of the

world and dominated by a colossal Atlas supporting a starry globe. Louis turned this into his throne room, and when he made a hurried departure he left behind a fine array of Imperial furniture and tapestries. There's also a fine collection of works by Dutch masters, commissioned by the town council during the 17th century. Rembrandt, who had fallen from favour with the council at the time, is conspicuous by his absence.

KONINKLIJK PALEIS;
Closed for refurbishment, scheduled to reopen 2009. www.koninkluikhuis.nl

5 Leaving the Royal Palace, turn right. Walk to the south side of the Dam, cross Paleisstraat, turn right again, then turn immediately left onto Nieuwezijds Voorburgwal. Follow this, keeping to the east side, for around 200yd (182m), and turn left into Sint Luciensteeg. At the end, turn right onto Kalverstraat, walk a further 50yd (46m) and look out for a venerable gateway set back into the wall on the right. This is the entrance to the Amsterdams Historisch Museum.

This is one of Amsterdam's oldest buildings. Built in the 15th century, it was first the Convent of St Lucia. In 1578, it was acquired by the city and became the municipal orphanage or Burgerweeshuis. The dove in the carved medallion above the entrance, symbolizing the Holy Spirit, dates from its time as a convent. The verse carved next to it, by Amsterdam's most famous poet, Joost van den Vondel (1587-1679), encourages passers-by to 'give a little support' by dropping a Euro or two into the collection box. Entering the museum, you cross two courtyards. As you walk through the first, the Boys' Courtyard, look out for the row of little alcoves on the left side, where the boys could store their possessions – even orphans, it seems, were relatively prosperous in Amsterdam's Golden Age. The entrance to the museum proper lies through the former Girls' Courtyard.

It takes at least 90 minutes to do justice to all 20 rooms. If time is short, it's worth entering the museum just to leave by way of the Schuttersgalerij, which leads to the exit. This roofed-in, narrow alley is hung with paintings commissioned by the militia companies formed in the

ABOVE: DAM SQUARE BY NIGHT

WHERE TO EAT

🍴 IN DE WILDEMAN,
Kolksteeg 3;
Tel: 020 638 2348.
More than 300 years old – and it
shows. 17 beers on tap, 200-plus in
bottles. Also serves snacks. €€

🍴 CAFÉ LUXEMBOURG,
Spui 24;
Tel: 020 620 6265.
Breakfast and snacks all day, wider
evening menu. Good wine list. €€€

🍴 HOPPE,
Spui 18;
Tel: 020 420 4420.
Typical 'brown café' (walls stained by
centuries of smoke), Hoppe opened
in 1670. Busy in the evening. €

14th century to maintain the peace and
defend the city. By the 17th century they
were prosperous enough to commission
the likes of Rembrandt and Hals to paint
their group portraits. Rembrandt's *Night
Watch* is, of course, the most famous. The
portraits in the Schuttersgalerij are by
lesser-known painters, but are still fun
– especially the jolly, almost comic-book-
style depictions of company banquets.

6 The Schuttersgalerij exits onto
Gedempte Begijnensloot. Turn right,
walk past the junctions of Waterstraat
and Rozenboomsteeg on your left and
the entrance to the Begijnhof courtyard
on your right, to Spui.

On Fridays, this cheery square is packed
with stalls selling antiquarian books;
on Sundays, it's taken over by the
Kunstmarkt, with booths selling prints,
paintings, sculpture and ceramics. In the
middle is one of Amsterdam's emblems:
'T Lieverdje (*The Little Darling*), an
impish bronze figure with arms akimbo,
stockings round his ankles and cap stuck
on the back of his head, who symbolizes
the city's spirit of resistance. The square
also has some excellent pubs and cafes
where you can stop for a rest and
refreshment at the end of the walk.

7 Take tram 1, 2 or 5 northbound to
return to Centraal Station.

A Taste of the Golden Age on Herengracht

Discover the elaborate houses of rich merchants who ornamented them in line with their increasing wealth as they traded all over the globe.

A decade of war from 1568-78 freed Amsterdam from the oppressive rule of Spain and ushered in the Golden Age. The city's biggest rival, Antwerp, had sided with Catholic Spain and been sacked by the Protestant rebels in 1585, and many of its inhabitants – including skilled artisans, painters and scholars – fled to Amsterdam. The city became a haven for scholarship and the arts, but it kept its feet firmly on the ground and its eyes on the money. With the ports of the Spanish Empire closed to Dutch trade, Amsterdam merchants found new routes. Commodities such as spices, sugar and tobacco made them rich, and the money trickled down to the craftsmen who built their luxurious townhouses along the new canals. By the mid-17th century, visitors from Paris and London were impressed by Amsterdam's prosperity, tidiness and public amenities such as streets lit by oil lamps. Wars with the envious English and French eventually ended the Golden Age, but much of its heritage can still be seen on this walk.

1 From Stationsplein, cross the Open Haven by whichever bridge is nearest and turn right on Prins Hendrikkade, the busy thoroughfare that runs along the waterfront. Follow this road to the meeting of the Singel canal and the Open Haven, cross the Singel by the bridge, and turn left, on Singel. Turn right at Haarlemmerstraat and cross two minor side streets to Herenmarkt.

Occupying most of the square is the Westindische Huis, the former headquarters of the Dutch West India Company. Set up in 1624, this trading venture made its pile by supplying African slaves to the colonies of the Caribbean. Its canny merchants also bought an island from the Manhattan Indians for beads and blankets and named it New Amsterdam, now, of course, New York. They lost it to the English in 1664.

2 Leave the square by Haarlemmerstraat, take the next left, and turn left again along the Brouwersgracht canal.

In medieval times, the Brouwersgracht or Brewer's Canal was lined with hundreds of small breweries that supplied homes and alehouses with beer, in those days a healthier drink than canal water. By the early 16th century, the canals were so filthy that water had to be shipped in to the city from the cleaner River Vecht.

3 At the next bridge, turn right, crossing the confluence of the Brouwersgracht and Herengracht.

This is one of the most-photographed canal scenes in Amsterdam, and as you walk you will be passed by boatloads of happy snappers.

The streets that run along either side of Amsterdam's many canals usually bear the same name as the canal. This means that an odd-numbered building may be on the opposite side of the canal from an even-numbered building on the same street. The three major canals that ring central Amsterdam – Herengracht, Keizersgracht and Prinsengracht – were all excavated in the early 17th century to drain marshland and create space for the city to expand. Houses were built on dozens of wooden pilings driven into the muddy ground. With time, these foundations have subsided, and most of the buildings along the canals tend to lean slightly drunkenly on their neighbours for support.

The Herengracht, or Gentleman's Canal, was where the richest merchants of the Golden Age lived, but the magnificence of their houses was for the most part confined to the inside. With land at a premium, even the wealthy were forced to build their homes tall and narrow, and puritanical Protestant Amsterdam in any case frowned on public shows of wealth – houses were taxed according to the width of their frontage. The beauty of these houses is in their gracious proportions and craftsmanship – given the technical challenges faced by the architects who designed them, it's amazing that the hundreds of historic buildings that line the Herengracht are still standing at all.

DISTANCE 3 miles (4.8km)

ALLOW 3 hours

START Stationsplein

FINISH Rembrandtplein

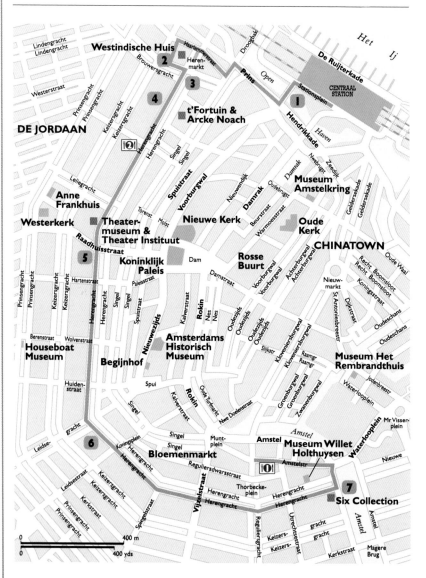

4 With the canal on your left, walk two blocks down the west side of Herengracht and cross the short bridge over the small Leliegracht, to Herengracht 168. On the way, look across the canal to the adjoining warehouses at No.s 43-45, on the opposite bank, known as 't Fortuin (the Fortune) and Arcke Noach (Noah's Ark). Built in 1600, they are the oldest buildings on the Herengracht.

House-owners of the Golden Age began to display their wealth with elaborately ornamented neck-gables, introduced by the architect Philips Vingboons (1608-78), whose work was very popular with Amsterdam's upper class. Earlier houses had simple step-gables and, as you walk along the Herengracht, you can see how gable ornamentation grew more elaborate as it became a status symbol. Vingboons added the first such gable to Herengracht 168 in 1638. Next door, at 170-172, the Bartolottihuis, with its grandiose façade of red brick and white plaster, was built in 1617 for a prosperous brewer, Willem van den Heuvel. At the time, it was the height of style to Italianize one's name; Willem changed his to Guillielmo Bartolotti. The two buildings now house the Amsterdam Theatre Institute (inside the Bartlottihuis) and Museum (at 168). The museum holds an eclectic collection of playbills and costumes.

AMSTERDAM THEATRE INSTITUTE AND MUSEUM;

MON-FRI 11-5, SAT-SUN 1-5

www.tin.nl

5 Turn left as you exit the museum, cross wide Raadhuisstraat and continue along Herengracht. Carry on for four blocks, crossing Hartenstraat, Wolvenstraat and Huidenstraat, and cross Leidsegracht. Between Radhuistraat and Leidsegracht, classic buildings of the Golden Age stand cheek by jowl on either side of the canal with more recent imitations from the 19th and 20th centuries. Herengracht canal soon starts to curve westward, to become the Gouden Bocht – variously translated as Golden Bend, Golden Bight or Golden Curve.

This stretch of Herengracht, between Koningsplein and Vijzelstraat, displays the wealth of the Golden Age most ostentatiously – hence its name. The houses here date from the late 17th century, when the wealthy could afford to buy double-width building lots, and

ABOVE: THE GRAND GABLES OF THE BARTOLOTTI HOUSE

WHERE TO EAT

🍴 CAFÉ SCHILLER/BRASSERIE
SCHILLER,
Rembrandtplein 36;
Tel: 020 624 9864.
Traditional Dutch and French dishes.
The next-door café serves snacks. €€

🍴 't ARENDSNEST,
Herengracht 90;
Tel: 020 421 2057.
www.arendsnest.nl
Beers from 50 Dutch breweries. €

build their *stadspaleisjes* – literally 'little town palaces' – in stone instead of brick. It's typical of Amsterdam at this time that they showed off their wealth by the costly materials they used, not by the kind of architectural frills and furbelows favoured by their contemporaries elsewhere in Europe. The most striking of all these houses – perhaps the most beautiful in Amsterdam – is No. 475, and it is a fascinating anomaly.

Most of the grandest surviving homes along the Herengracht are 18th-century conversions of 17th-century buildings. The first house on this site was built for the merchant Denys Nuyts in 1672. Sixty years later it was demolished and an entirely new building was commissioned by Petronella van Lennep de Neufville (1688-1749), the wealthy widow of a cloth magnate. The architect was Daniel Marot (1661-1752). Marot is credited with bringing the French Louis XIV style to Amsterdam, and Petronella clearly

gave him a big budget to work with. Ionic columns, Corinthian pilasters and caryatids festoon the frontage. Petronella's descendants went on to become one of Amsterdam's biggest theatrical families. They lived here until 1792, when the house was sold to the wealthy merchant and art collector Jan Gildemeester, who turned the ground floor into a showcase for his own collection of paintings. The Rijksmuseum has a painting (*Jan Gildemeester in his Art Gallery, 1794/95*) by Adriaan de Lelie, which portrays Jan and his guests; he is clearly very proud of his home. Today, No. 475 is the Amsterdam branch of a Russian bank. The ghosts of the hard-headed merchants who built their homes on the Herengracht would probably approve.

6 Carry on round the Bend for six short blocks, crossing, on your right, Leidsestraat, Spiegelstraat, Vijzelstraat, the short (and much-photographed) bridge over the Reguliersgracht, and Utrechtsetraat. Continue to the end of Herengracht, where it meets the Amstel river. At the end of the sixth block is the Six Collection.

Jan Six (1618-1700), best known as a patron of Rembrandt (who painted his portrait in 1654), lived at Herengracht 619. Six personifies 17th-century Amsterdam: son of a wealthy textile merchant, he moved on from trade to become a lawyer, politician and patron of the arts. In 1655, he married Margaretha, daughter of Nicholas Tulp, the burgomaster mayor of Amsterdam,

and became part of the establishment, becoming mayor himself at the age of 73. His descendants are still major movers and shakers on the Dutch cultural scene.

The Jan Six collection can be visited only by appointment, with a letter of introduction arranged through the Rijksmuseum (www.rijksmuseum.nl): you will need to present your passport.

7 Turn right, then left, over the bridge that crosses the confluence of the Herengracht and the Amstel. Continue past the north bank of the Herengracht on your left, take the next left onto Amstelstraat, and walk one short block to Rembrandtplein. Full of cafés, this is a good place for a rest. Trams 4, 9 and 25 take you back to Stationsplein.

Secret Chapels and Hiding Places

Amsterdam's reputation for tolerance isn't new – for centuries it's been a safe haven for minorities fleeing religious persecution.

As long ago as the 16th century, Amsterdam welcomed Jews and Protestants fleeing the genocidal world of the Holy Roman Empire. During the German occupation of World War II, underground resistance groups helped to shelter Jews and other fugitives in the city. From the 1960s onward, Amsterdam became a world capital of the counter–culture. That easy-going attitude prevails: the best cannabis in the world is enjoyed in the salubrious surroundings of the city's 'coffee shops', the gay scene (for men and women) thrives, and commercial sex is open and regulated. By and large, that reputation for tolerance is well earned, though it has its cynical side. For some 400 years, Amsterdam has tolerated just about anything that doesn't interfere with business – from live sex shows and the open enjoyment of certain herbs to the celebration of marriage vows between men and men, and women and women. But it hasn't always been as easy-going as it appears to be today. The best day for this walk is Saturday, when you can enjoy the Boerenmarkt at its best. Start early.

1 From Stationsplein, cross the Open Haven by whichever bridge is nearest and turn right on Prins Hendrikkade, the busy and rather dull thoroughfare that runs along the waterfront. Follow this to the meeting of the Singel canal and the Open Haven, cross the Singel by the first bridge you reach, turn left then second right and follow Brouwersgracht until it meets Prinsengracht.

You stand now on Papeneiland, and the name itself is your first hint that Amsterdam wasn't always as tolerant as it seems. The name means Island of the Papists. There is no remnant of the Carthusian monastery that once stood here and gave the island its name.

2 Now cross Prinsengracht by Lekkeresluis. The Noorderkerk looms on your right as you walk down the west bank of Prinsengracht. Walk down half a block, and turn right into Noordermarkt.

The Noorderkerk was built in 1620. Its designer was Hendrick de Keyser, the star architect of Amsterdam's Golden Age. This massive, bulky church was his last big project. It's a solid lump of brown brick and grey slate, and it departs completely from the old Catholic architectural tradition: it has no nave, transept, choir or altar. Instead, de Keyser reverted to the older style of the Orthodox basilica – four equal arms radiating out from a central space. But he couldn't resist crowning it with one of his trademark spires.

The Noordermarkt, the cobbled square in front of the church, was the place of one of the city's livestock markets. On Saturdays, it's still the venue for the weekly Boerenmarkt (Farmers' Market – for more on the market see Walk 10).

3 Another of de Keyser's churches, the Westerkerk, is your next landmark. Walk on down Prinsengracht to the next bridge (Prinsenstraat). Turn left across the bridge, then immediately right. With the canal on your right, carry on across the Leliegracht bridge and join the line to enter the Anne Frank Huis at Prinsengracht 263.

The Frank family fled Germany for Amsterdam in 1933, just after the election of Adolf Hitler's Nazi government. Seven years later, the Germans arrived. Anne Frank's diary was published in 1947, three years after she and her family had been betrayed to the Germans and sent to the Bergen–Belsen death camp. Anne died there, of typhus, aged 16. The Franks lived in this tiny apartment, hidden behind a false wall in her father's spice warehouse, from June 1942 until August 1944, when a Dutch neighbour sold them out to the occupiers and their collaborators. She began her diary just before they went into hiding. It was found by an office cleaner in 1946. Her father, Otto, was the only member of the Frank family to survive the German extermination camps.

ANNE FRANKHUIS;
DAILY; SEE WEBSITE FOR TIMES
www.annefrank.org

DISTANCE 3 miles (4.8km)

ALLOW 4 hours

START Stationsplein

FINISH Stationsplein

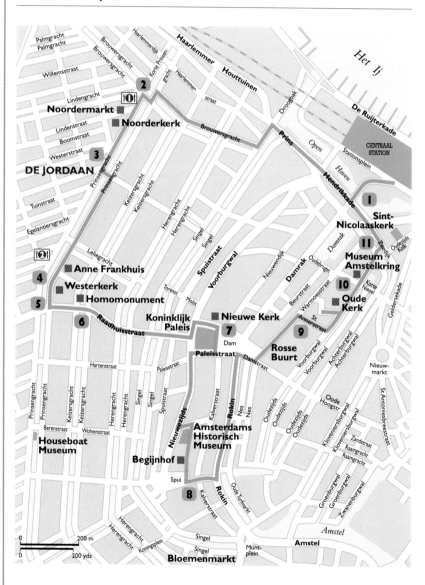

4 Leaving the Anne Frank house, turn left. The globe-crowned spire of the Westerkerk (the tallest church tower in Amsterdam) looms above you.

The Westerkerk is the prettiest building in Amsterdam, and it is riddled with hidden histories. In its day, it was the biggest Protestant church in the world. Hendrick de Keyser designed it, in 1619, but it wasn't finished until 1638. Hendrick died before the job was done, and his son Pieter completed it. The grandiloquent globe-and-crown that tops the Westertoren is the contribution of Pieter's colleague, Cornelis Dancker. It's a piece of sheer architectural one-upmanship: Amsterdam had been granted the right to this imperial symbol by the Holy Roman Emperor Maximilian in 1489 – a century before the Dutch sent his Spaniards packing.

In front of you as you enter is the magnificent organ, decorated by Gerard de Lairesse (1641-1711), a pupil of Rembrandt. On your right, a plaque marks the tomb of Rembrandt's son, Titus. And somewhere underneath your feet lie the bones of Rembrandt van Rijn himself.

The Westerkerk's bell sets the time for old Amsterdam, ringing every hour and half-hour, and from midday-13.00 on Sundays. Take the time to slog to the top of the Westertoren steeple – it's just under 280ft (85m) tall – for the best view of the old city centre.

WESTERKERK;
MON-FRI 11-3 www.westerkerk.nl

5 Turn left as you exit the church, and almost immediately turn left again on Raadhuisstraat. Carry on for one short block to the corner of Raadhuisstraat and Keizersgracht.

Just north of the Raadhuistraat bridge, two triangles of pink granite

WHERE TO EAT

📷 CAFÉ PAPENEILAND,
Prinsengracht 2;
Tel: 020 624 1989.
This 'brown café' claims to be the
oldest in Amsterdam; it's been here
since 1642. €

📷 CAFÉ CHRIS,
Prisengracht and Bloemstraat;
Tel: 020 624 5942.
Traces its ancestry all the way back
to 1624, when the Westerkerk was
being built. €

are inlaid into the pavement. A third
juts into the canal. These comprise
the Homomonument, designed by
Karin Daan and installed in 1987 to
commemorate the gay men and women
imprisoned and murdered by the Nazis
during World War II, as well as people
who are still persecuted today for their
sexual orientation, and to honour those
who continue to struggle for gay rights
everywhere. Engraved in the stone are
the words *Naar vriendschaap zulk een
mateloos verlangen* (*Such an endless desire
for friendship*) – a line from the poem
To a Young Fisherman, by Jacob Israel de
Haan (1881-1924).

6 Cross the bridge and continue along
Raadhuisstraat, crossing bridges
over the Herengracht and the Singel.
Raadhuistraat ends at the Royal Palace.
Cross Nieuwezijds Voorburgwal, turn
left, then at the north corner of the

Palace turn right into Moses en
Aaron-straat. The Nieuwe Kerk is
opposite the Palace, on the north
side of this street.

New? Not very. The first church on the
site was built in the late 15th century
but was several times destroyed by
fire and restored. The vaulted interior,
with its skilfully carved Baroque pulpit
and stained-glass windows, dates from
the 17th century. This is Amsterdam's
equivalent of London's Westminster
Cathedral: the place where Dutch
monarchs are crowned, and the great and
the good lie buried – among them the
greatest of Dutch poets, Joost van den
Vondel (1587-1679). He lived to be 92
years old, no mean feat in the perilous
17th century.

7 Leaving the Nieuwe Kerk, go back
to the Palace and turn right. Walk
to the south side of the Dam, cross
Paleisstraat, turn right again, then turn
immediately left onto Nieuwezijds
Voorburgwal. Follow this, keeping to the
east side, for around 200yd (183m), and
turn left into Sint Luciensteeg. Bypass
the Amsterdams Historish Museum, and
enter Gedempte Begijnensloot. Walk
past the junctions of Waterstraat and
Rozenboomsteeg on your left and find
the tiny gateway to the Begijnhof on
your right.

The gateway leads into a courtyard
crammed with hidden histories. The
Netherlands has many *hofjes* (almshouses)
and this is the finest of all. It was built

in 1346 as a sanctuary for the Begijnen, a group of unmarried women who lived as a religious community but without taking nuns' vows. They devoted themselves to caring for the poor and the sick. The almshouses surround a calm, cobbled garden square, which is dominated by the Begijnkerk. This church, built in 1419, was confiscated from the Catholic Begijns during the Protestant Reformation in 1578. In 1607 it was given to Amsterdam's expatriate Scottish Presbyterian community. Since then, confusingly, it has been known as the Engelse Kerk or English Church.

The interior is typically plain, but the pulpit panels are the work of the avant-garde artist Piet Mondriaan (1872-1944).

The house at Begijnhof 34 stands out from its neighbours. It's one of only two wooden houses left in Amsterdam. The city council banned wooden buildings in 1521 after a series of disastrous fires ravaged the city. Next to it stands the 'secret' chapel in which the Begijns continued to worship, discreetly, until religious tolerance was restored in 1795.

BEGIJNHOF;

DAILY; 9-5 www.begijnhofamsterdam.nl

8 Gedempte Begijnensloot leads to the Spui. Turn left, and walk one block to Rokin. Turn left on this busy shopping street and follow it all the way back to the Dam. Turn right on Damstraat, then immediately left on Warmoesstraat.

This is the oldest street in the city. Its residents have included the Spanish tyrant, the Duke of Alva, in 1574; the poet Vondel, in the late 17th century; the Mozart family in 1766; and Karl Marx in the 1850s. These days, sadly, it's a rather tatty mix of porn stores, souvenir shops and sleazy bars.

9 Turn right into St Annenstraat, and after about 55yd (50m) turn left, along the west side of the Oudezijds Voorburgwal canal. Take the next left and walk another 55yd (50m) to the Oude Kerk, which dwarfs the buildings around it.

This is Amsterdam's oldest church and one of its oldest buildings. The Gothic tower dates from 1306, although its 220ft (67m) tall wooden steeple was added later, in 1566, and most of the rest of the church was rebuilt around the same time. Its splendid altars were destroyed during the Reformation, but three stained-glass windows dating from 1555 survive in the Chapel of Our Lady. Rembrandt's wife, Saskia, has her tomb on the north side of the church.

10 Turn left as you leave the church, passing from the sacred to the profane. Oudezijds Voorburgwal is on the fringes of the red light district, as evidenced by the scantily clad women sitting in shop windows along the street. Follow this street to No. 40.

The Museum Amstelkring is hidden behind the façade of an inconspicuous 17th-century canal-side house. With the triumph of Protestantism in 1578, Catholic churches throughout the city were closed or converted, and Catholic forms of worship were prohibited. In 1661, Jan Hartman, a wealthy Catholic merchant, built his shop and home here, and converted the two upper floors of his and the two adjoining buildings into a *schuilkerk* – a 'secret' church. There were many of these, but this is the only one which has been fully preserved. It's reached by a series of vertiginous narrow stairs, at the top of which is, not a dusty attic, but a magnificent church with space for up to 200 worshippers. It is splendidly furnished with religious statuary and silverware, paintings and a vast organ – along with a collapsible altar that could be whisked out of sight if the church was in danger of being raided. It is unlikely that such a huge space could really have been secret (any more than the little chapel of the Begijns), so it seems that once the first blaze of Protestant reforming fervour had died down, the authorities agreed to tolerate Catholic worship in private.

MUSEUM AMSTELKRING;
MON-SAT 10-5 SUN 1-5
www.museumamstelkring.nl

11 Carrying on to the north end of Oudezijds Voorburgwal will bring you to Zeedijk and the twin towers of the Sint-Nicolaaskerk. Turn left here and in less than 100yd (91m) you will find yourself back on Prins Hendrikkade, in front of Centraal Station, where you can catch any tram or metro.

Art and Antiques on the Inner Canals

Ever since its Golden Age, Amsterdam has been a city of artists. Many visitors go home with a painting from one of the Sunday markets.

It wasn't just the wealthy who bought paintings of canalside scenes or portraits of their families to hang on their walls. Not everyone could afford a Rembrandt: but for every great master there were dozens of hack painters turning out acceptable simulations at a fraction of the price. In some ways, that hasn't changed. Amsterdam is still full of grand commercial galleries that cater to those with very deep pockets – but its back streets and open-air markets still offer the hope of a bargain that you can afford, whether it's an antique tin toy, a pop-art poster from the 1960s or a new print, painting or piece of sculpture from one of Amsterdam's still-to-be-discovered talents. The best day for this walk is a Sunday, when open-air art markets are held on Spui and Thorbeckeplein.

Start this walk on the south side of Westermarkt – take tram 13, 14 or 17. Walk less than a dozen yards west to Prinsengracht. Turn left and then walk along Prinsengracht, crossing Raadhuisstraat and Reestraat. At Berenstraat, cross the canal, then cross to the west side of Prinsengracht, and enter Elandsgracht. The Looier Antiquemarkt is at No. 109.

This is the largest permanent, indoor antiques market in the Netherlands and it's heaven for serious collectors, dabblers or just window-shoppers, with more than 70 stands and shops and 90 display cabinets. You'll find glassware, porcelain, gold and silver, prints and paintings, clocks and mirrors, furniture, dolls and tin toys. It's far from cheap – but on Wednesdays and at weekends De Looier hosts a less formal flea market where you might find a bargain if you get there early.
LOOIER ANTIQUEMARKT;
SAT-THU 11-5 www.looier.nl

2 Walk to the west end of Elandsgracht, turn left, and after one short block cross Looiersgracht to its south side. The entrance to the Rommelmarkt is close to the corner, at Looiersgracht 38.

You'll certainly find something you can afford in this ramshackle flea-market, but will you want to buy? Old records, CDs and tapes, cameras and binoculars, toys and games, cutlery and crockery abound – it's almost a museum of fads, fashions and dubious popular taste, going all the

WHERE TO EAT

|○| BRASSERIE BRATZ,
Elandsgracht 109;
Tel: 020 624 9038.
Friendly small brasserie bar inside De Looier antiques market. €

|○| DANTE,
Spuistraat 320;
Tel: 020 638 88 39.
Bar, restaurant and art gallery. Terrace overlooking the Singel. €€

|○| CAFÉ DANTZIG,
Stopera Building, Zwanenbrugwal 15;
Tel: 020 620 9039.
Part of the Stopera complex which houses the opera house. €€

way back to the 1960s and beyond.
ROMMELMARKT;
DAILY 11-5

3 Walk back along Looiersgracht in the direction of Prinsengracht. Cross the canal, walk along Runstraat and its eastern continuation, Huidenstraat, crossing Keizersgracht, Herengracht and Singel, to the Spui.

On a Friday, this cobbled square is jammed with stalls selling antiquarian books (mainly Dutch) and old prints. On a Sunday it's equally packed with stalls selling everything from surrealist works in oil and acrylic to ceramics and screenprints. Quality and price vary tremendously, but it's always worth a look.

31

DISTANCE **4 miles (6.4km)**

ALLOW **All day**

START **Westermarkt**

FINISH **Waterlooplein (tram 4, 9, 14 and Metro) or Stopera (Museum Boat)**

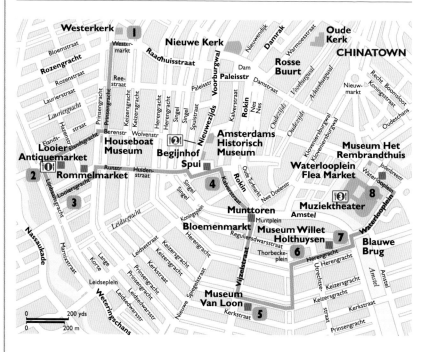

Leave the Spui by Kalverstraat, on the south side of the square, and follow this narrow street for two blocks to Muntplein, where the 17th-century Munttoren (Mint Tower), designed by the ubiquitous Hendrick de Keyser (1565-1621), is an unmistakable landmark. Cross Muntplein and the Singel Canal (look to your right for the floating stalls of the famous Bloemenmarkt, crammed with flowers, as you cross the bridge). Now walk down Vijzelstraat, a broad and unexciting shopping street, crossing Reguliersdwarsstraat, Herengracht and Keizersgracht. Turn left after crossing Keizersgracht and walk to Keizersgracht 672, close to the corner.

The first resident of this imposing 17th-century mansion was Ferdinand Bol (1616-80), one of Rembrandt's best-known pupils, but it is better known as the family home of one of Amsterdam's wealthiest dynasties. The van Loons started from fairly humble beginnings,

owning windmills in the Middle Ages. In 1602 Willem van Loon was a founder of the Dutch East India Company. In the early 19th century the van Loons were raised to the Dutch nobility, and the last resident of the house, Thora van Loon-Egidius, was chief lady-in-waiting to Queen Wilhelmina. She died in 1945, and after a painstaking restoration the house opened as a museum in 1973. The van Loon family are still closely involved with the running it. The mansion's 19th-century interior is virtually unchanged, and a monument to gracious living, with grand salons and halls hung with family portraits that reveal the van Loons' importance in the city's economic and political life. The house's biggest surprise is its large formal garden, which was laid out in the 1970s to a 17th-century plan, and restored in 1998 by the landscape architect Eugenie Andre de la Porte.

MUSEUM VAN LOON;

MAR-MAY, JUL-AUG WED-MON 11-5; rest of year FRI-MON 11-5 www.museumvanloon.nl

5 Exiting the house, turn right, walk along Keizersgracht to the Reguliersgracht bridge, and walk up this quiet, narrow canal, re-crossing the Keizersgracht and Herengracht canals. Just after crossing the Herengracht, you find yourself on Thorbeckeplein.

The statue in the middle of the square is of Johan Rudolf Thorbecke, the 19th-century liberal politician who reformed the Dutch electoral system in 1849. On Sundays in spring and summer, it's the venue for an open-air modern art market, with around 25 painters and printmakers showing their work. Quality, it has to be said, varies – and not all the 350,000 visitors who come here every year appear impressed. You have to admire the artists' courage in exposing their work to a sometimes philistine audience.

MODERN ART MARKET;

SUN 9-5 www.modern-art-market.nl

6 About face, go back to the north bank of Herengracht, turn left and walk one and a half blocks along the canal, past the Utrechtsestraat bridge, to Herengracht 605.

Built in 1687, this is another beautifully preserved mansion, graced by a superb collection of furniture and porcelain – the legacy of its 19th-century owners, Abraham Willet and Louisa Geertruida Holthuysen, who left the house and their vast collection of antiques to the city. The rooms are gorgeous, especially the Louis XVI dining room. Abraham's collection of Delft ware is displayed in a pretty little bedroom overlooking the hidden garden. His taste in paintings was less refined – few of those displayed are worth a second look. Louisa inherited the house from her wealthy father in 1858 and married the less wealthy Abraham three years later; they then set out to spend a large chunk of Louisa's inheritance on redecorating in opulent style. The couple were childless (there is a rumour, never verified, that Louisa was in fact hermaphrodite). Abraham died in 1888 and Louisa, who died seven years later. Her will insisted that the museum should bear both their names and that Abraham's art collection should remain on display. The museum's first curator, Frans Coenen, fictionalized the couple in his novel *Onpersoonlijke Herinneringen (Impersonal Memories)*, published in 1936. It shows the husband (also called Abraham) using his wife's fortune to indulge his expensive tastes.

MUSEUM WILLET HOLTHUYSEN;

MON-FRI 10-5, SAT-SUN 11-5
www.willetholthuysen.nl

7 From the museum, turn left onto Herengracht and walk half a short block to the west bank of the Amstel river. Turn left, and only a few steps away is the famous Blauwe Brug (Blue Bridge). Cross the bridge, and once on the other side, cross the street. On your left is the huge Muziektheater arts complex. Walk past this, and turn left among the colourful stalls of the Waterlooplein Flea Market.

The art and antiques to be found in this hippy-dippy open-air market are definitely of the counter-cultural persuasion. If you have a collector's eye for vintage vinyl, want to supplement your wardrobe with an antique leather jacket or an array of ethnic accessories, or are looking for authentic 1960s psychedelic art, this is the place to come.

WATERLOOPLEIN FLEA MARKET;

MON-FRI 9-5, SAT 8.30-5.30

8 The flea market is a handy place to end this walk. Nearby, there are plenty of bars and cafes where you can admire (or regret) your purchases, and you have a choice of metro, tram and Museum Boat services.

Maritime Connections in and around Chinatown

Amsterdam once ruled the waves from Cape Town to Indonesia. See the tower where women waved their men off on long sea voyages.

Oddly enough, it's easy to forget or ignore Amsterdam's maritime history. When you arrive, the open water of the River Ij is invisible from the city centre, hidden behind the mass of Centraal Station. But the Ij is Amsterdam's corridor to the sea – and in the city's heyday it was the gateway to a maritime world that stretched from North America to the East Indies and has left its stamp on the city. The *Verenigde Oostindische Compagnie* (Dutch East India Company), founded in 1602, built a trading empire that grew to include colonies in Cape Town, Ceylon (now Sri Lanka), India and, most of all, the East Indies – present-day Indonesia. By 1669, the VOC was wealthier and more powerful than most national governments, with its own navy of 40 warships, a merchant fleet of 150 vessels, and an army of 10,000, but by the late 18th century it could no longer stand up to the British. Dutch sea power never really recovered after the Napoleonic Wars, during which the Netherlands picked the losing side, but the Dutch empire continued to expand in the East Indies well into the 20th century.

With the station behind you, cross the Open Haven (so called because it opens onto the broader reaches of the River Ij, hidden from view behind Centraal Station), to Prins Hendrikkade, and turn left. The Sint-Nicolaaskerk is an unmistakable landmark, occupying the block between Prins Hendrikkade, Zeedijk and Oudezijds Kolk.

Prins Hendrik (1820–79), after whom this long and busy waterfront is named, was the third son of Willem II and earned his soubriquet of The Navigator for his fascination with maritime matters. But by his time, the Netherlands was no longer a great naval power. For 200 years, it had been more than capable of challenging Spain, England and France at sea, but Dutch sea power never really recovered from the destruction of the fleet by the Royal Navy at Camperdown in 1797, during the Dutch alliance with revolutionary France.

The Sint-Nicolaaskerk – Amsterdam's biggest and ugliest Catholic church – was built between 1875 and 1887 and is dedicated to St Nicholas, patron saint of merchants and seafarers.

2 Walk past the Sint-Nicolaaskerk to the corner of Geldersekade, where one of Amsterdam's oldest buildings overlooks the canal.

The Schreierstoren or Weepers Tower is the last remaining bastion of the old city walls. Amsterdam women traditionally gathered here to watch their sons, husbands and sweethearts set off on

WHERE TO EAT

🍴 LATEI,
Zeedijk 143;
Tel: 020 625 7485.
Tiny, funky combination of antique shop and café-restaurant. €

🍴 CAFÉ RESTAURANT IN DE WAAG,
Nieuwmarkt 4;
Tel: 020 422 7772.
www.indewaag.nl
Housed in the medieval weigh-house or *Waag* on Nieuwmarkt. €

🍴 CAFÉ DE DRUIF,
Rapenburgplein 83;
Tel: 020 624 4530.
Ancient café by the canal, serving beer, *geniever* (gin-type spirit) and snacks. €

years-long voyages to Asia, Africa and the Americas. The gablestone shows wailing womenfolk, and a plaque commemorates Henry Hudson, the British navigator who set off from here in 1609 (under contract from the VOC) to seek a sea route from the Atlantic to the Pacific by way of North America. He didn't find it, but he did find the river on the east coast of America that still bears his name – and his exploration led to the founding of Nieuw Amsterdam, now New York.

3 About face, and turn left into Oudezijds Kolk. With the Sint-Nicolaaskerk on your right, walk up this narrow street to Zeedijk and turn left.

37

DISTANCE	**3 miles (4.8km)**
ALLOW	**3 hours**
START	**Stationsplein**
FINISH	**Stationsplein**

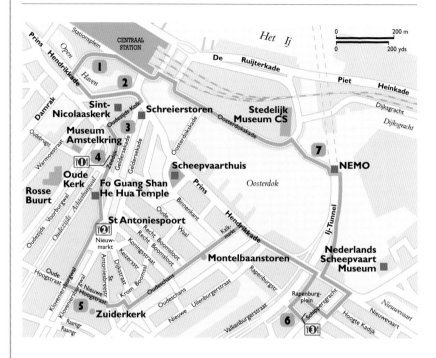

The Zeedijk was once part of the city's sea wall (which is what its name means) but land reclamation throughout some three centuries means it's now a full block back from the waterfront. Merging with the red-light district, this is the most ethnically diverse part of the city centre – it's often referred to as Amsterdam's Chinatown, but shops, restaurants and faces reflect every aspect of the city's colonial heritage. There are Indonesian, Thai, Indian, Surinamese and Caribbean stores and restaurants, as well as Chinese

establishments. Many of the Chinese people who settled here did not come directly from China. The former Dutch East Indies had a large ethnic Chinese minority. After independence, when the colony became Indonesia, many of them left, especially after anti-Chinese pogroms in the mid-1960s, when thousands of Chinese were killed by Indonesian mobs.

The most prominent of Zeedijk's Asian links is the Fo Gang Sha He Hua Temple, at Zeedijk 106-118. Completed in 2000, it's often described as 'the largest

Buddhist temple in Europe', but that is a little misleading. There aren't very many Buddhist temples in Europe, and this one is quite unassuming – especially compared with Amsterdam's vast Christian churches. The triple entrance gate is in traditional Chinese Buddhist style, with a central gateway for monks and nuns, flanked by smaller entrances for lay visitors.

4 Follow Zeedijk through the heart of Chinatown to Nieuwmarkt. Keep heading in the same direction, across the square (passing the red-brick St Antoniespoort, built in 1488, on your left) and walk down Kloveniersburgwal, keeping the canal on your left. When you reach Oude Hoogstraat (third on your right after leaving Nieuwmarkt), turn left across the canal bridge and pause midway across.

Look back across the canal from the south side of the bridge. The massive, warehouse-like brick building that faces you is the Oostindischehuis, the former headquarters of the Dutch East India Company. Considering the company's enormous wealth, it's a very plain building – its only embellishment is the VOC coat of arms on the pediment. The tall double doors once gave access to cavernous storerooms on each floor.

39

5 Cross the bridge and walk along Nieuwe Hoogstraat, crossing St Anthoniesbreestraat, until you reach Oudeschans. On reaching the canal, the street jinks briefly right. Keep following the waterside all the way to the end of Oudeschans, and when you reach Prins Hendrikkade turn right to cross the canal, staying on the righthand side of the bridge. Pause as you cross, and look back down the canal for a glimpse of two of Hendrick de Keyser's (1565-1621) fancy trademark towers, the Montelbaanstoren about halfway down Oudeschans on the west side, and the Zuiderkerk a little further south. Carry on eastward, cross the bridge over the Valkenburgerstraat dual carriageway and the entrance to the Ij-Tunnel that carries traffic beneath the river, and on the other side of the bridge, turn immediately right onto Nieuwe Foeliestraat, then left again onto Rapenburgplein.

On the corner of this canalside square at No. 83, the Café de Druif opened in 1631. It is claimed that Piet Heyn, the Dutch commander who earned a place in history by capturing a Spanish silver fleet in 1628, sometimes drank here. He lived nearby, at No. 13, but as he died in 1629, at the age of 50, this seems unlikely. Knock back a *borrel* of geniever in his honour anyway, before you carry on.

6 From the eastern corner of Rapenburgplein, cross Schippersgracht. The artificial island on which you now stand once hummed with commerce. Along its inner side, the Entrepotdok was a solid mass of bonded warehouses. Since the 1990s, these have been converted into yuppie apartments. At the end of the bridge, turn left on Kadiksplein, pass Hoogte Kadijk on your right, to arrive back at Prins Hendrikkade. Cross to the waterfront. The futuristic building ahead of you and to your left, at the tip of the manmade Ij-Tunnel peninsula which juts into the Oosterdok, is the NEMO Centre. To your right, across a harbour bristling with the masts of historic vessels, you will see a huge and imposing 17th-century building. Originally the arsenal of the Dutch Navy, this is now the Nederlands Scheepvaart Museum (Netherlands Maritime Museum).

The museum is closed for renovation and due to reopen in mid 2009. In the meantime, its most striking exhibit, the *Amsterdam*, is moored at the NEMO Centre. This 148ft (48m) three-masted sailing ship is a near-perfect replica of the original *Amsterdam*, a Dutch East Indiaman that foundered off the south coast of England in 1749. Built in the 1980s, the *Amsterdam* is crewed by actors who bring the heyday of the Dutch maritime empire to life. It's a great place to finish this walk.

7 From the west side of the NEMO Centre, cross the Oosterdok by the footbridge to Oosterdokskade and with the harbour on your left, walk back to Stationsplein, a 5-10 minute stroll, where you can pick up a tram or the metro.

Jewish Amsterdam

In the early 17th century Amsterdam became a haven for Jews escaping persecution. This walk traces their considerable influence on the city.

The Inquisition in Spain and Portugal forced Sephardic Jews to flee. Many of the earliest to arrive in Amsterdam were *Marranos* – Jews who had been forced to convert to the Catholic faith but who remained secretly Jewish. In Amsterdam they were able to return to their true faith. Soon after, Ashkenazi Jews fleeing persecution in Russia and Poland also sought refuge in Amsterdam. Many Sephardim were already prosperous when they arrived; most Ashkenazim were broke, and found it much tougher to get a foot on the ladder to prosperity – especially as they were not allowed to join the guilds of skilled craftsmen. Jews finally gained equal rights during the revolutionary Batavian Republic in 1796 (see Walk 7), but most still struggled to make a living until the 19th century, when the diamond trade created a demand for skilled artisans. Although Amsterdam never had a ghetto in the literal sense, the eastern part of the city, from the Oudeschans to what is now Waterlooplein, was the heart of the Jewish community, as evidenced by many street names.

Take the metro to Nieuwmarkt. From the south corner of Nieuwmarkt, take St Antoniesbreestraat. Walk all the way down the right-hand side of this busy modern shopping street, past the Zuiderkerk, to No. 69.

Enter the Huis de Pinto for a glimpse of the opulent style in which wealthier Jewish families lived during the 17th century. The building is now a branch of the Amsterdam Public Library so admission is free. It was built in 1680, in Italian Renaissance style, for Isaac de Pinto, whose family had fled from Lisbon to Amsterdam in 1492. Look up, and prepare to be impressed by the splendid painted ceilings.

2 Continue in the same direction down St Antoniesbreestraat until you reach St Antonies Sluis (St Anthony's Bridge). Don't cross the canal here, but turn left. Keeping the water of Oudeschans on your right, turn left again, then immediately right, right again and left. Oudeschans still has its complement of houseboats, and in spring it is also dotted with the floating nests of great crested grebes and coots. Still with the canal on your right, walk four short blocks, passing on your left the corners of Keizersstraat, Koningsstraat, Recht Boomsloot and Oude Waal to the Montelbaanstoren, the most prominent landmark on this canal.

The Montelbaanstoren was originally part of the city defences, though you wouldn't guess this from its fanciful

WHERE TO EAT

[O] CAFÉ DE SLUYSWACHT,
Jodenbreestraat 1;
Tel: 020 625 7611.
www.sluyswacht.nl
Pleasant, light café with canalside terrace, serving drinks and a good choice of salads, quiches, tapas and snacks. €€

[O] JOODS HISTORISCHES MUSEUM CAFÉ,
JD Meierplein 2-4;
Tel: 020 531 0310.
www.jhm.nl
The museum café serves typical Amsterdam and international kosher dishes ranging from ginger cake to humus and gefilte fish. It also has five screens where you can browse the museum website. €

appearance. It was built in 1521, but a century later Hendrick de Keyser (1565-1621), architect of the Zuiderkerk, Westerkerk and Noorderkerk, got his hands on it and added one of his trademark steeples and an octagonal upper storey. These additions proved too much for the original foundations, and the tower began to lean towards the canal until, in a feat of engineering typical of Amsterdam, it was hauled back to the vertical and reinforced. It was a favourite subject for Rembrandt, who lived just across the Oudeschans, and it also became a meeting-point for Jewish refugees arriving in the city.

DISTANCE **4 miles (6.4km)**

ALLOW **4 hours**

START **Nieuwmarkt**

FINISH **Nieuwmarkt**

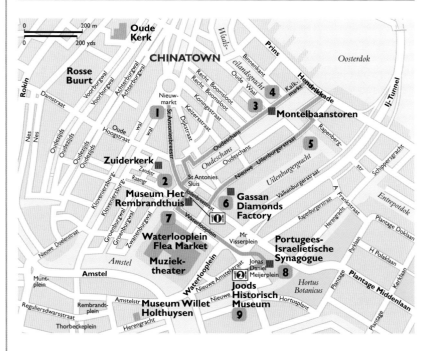

3 Before walking on along Oudeschans, cross the street to the house immediately opposite the tower and look up at the gablestones.

These show a toga-clad Roman emperor and empress – a visual pun on the architect's name, de Keyser (ie, Caesar).

4 Return to the canal side, turn left, and cross the Waalseilandsgracht bridge (there are lots of houseboats moored here). Continue to busy Prins

Hendrikkade, turn right, cross the bridge and at the east end turn first right into Peperstraat. The name of this street (Pepper Street) is a reminder that the buildings were originally the spice warehouses of the Dutch East India Company. Most have now been converted into offices, studios and apartments. Peperstraat is very short – at the end, turn left along the canalside, then almost immediately first right across Peperbrug. This brings you to the north end of Nieuwe Uilenburgerstraat.

From the 16th century on, this was the main thoroughfare of the Uilenburg island district, a maze of narrow alleys and slum housing that was home to many of the city's poorer Jews. Some families lived 10 to a room, with no sanitation.

5 Carry on to the southern end and the Gassan Diamonds factory, on your left at No. 173-175, just before the junction with Uilenburgergracht.

Built in 1879 by the Boas family, the factory with its 357 steam-driven wheels was literally at the cutting edge of the diamond industry, using the latest steam-powered technology and employing hundreds of skilled workers. Amsterdam's diamond trade began in the early 17th century, when Sephardic Jewish exiles arrived in the city from Spanish-ruled Antwerp. Many were already involved in diamond dealing, and they recruited cutters and polishers from the growing Jewish community. Jewish workers were still barred from most Amsterdam trade guilds, and they came to excel in this new skill. The introduction of steam-driven machinery in the mid-19th century and the discovery of huge new diamond fields in South Africa in 1869 boosted business still further, making Amsterdam the diamond capital of the world until the German occupation of 1940-45 and the mass murder of the Jewish community by the Nazis. Today, the diamond business is still important – but Amsterdam once again plays second fiddle to Antwerp.

GASSAN DIAMOND FACTORY,
DAILY 9-5 www.gassandiamonds.nl

6 Cross the canal and walk down Uilenburgersteeg to reach Jodenbreestraat, second on your right; turn right and walk one block to the north end of this busy and rather characterless thoroughfare which was once the bustling heart of the Jewish quarter. When you reach the canal, turn left and – staying on the opposite side of the street from the canal – walk about halfway down the block to the Rembrandthuis at No. 4-6.

Rembrandt van Rijn (1606-69), to give him his full name, bought this red-shuttered house in 1639, by which time he was already a well-established artist and had made a profitable marriage to the wealthy Saskia van Uylenburg. The people of the Jewish districts nearby

ABOVE: EXTERIOR OF THE REMBRANDTHUIS MUSEUM

provided Rembrandt with inspiration and models for many of his paintings. He lived here for 20 years, but in later life his work fell from favour with the public, he went bankrupt and the house was sold. It's been brilliantly restored – there's a recreation of a 17th-century cabinet of curiosities and more than 250 of his drawings and etchings on display. Allow plenty of time to absorb it all.

REMBRANDTHUIS;

SAT-THU 10-5, FRI 10-9 www.rembrandthuis.nl

7 Ahead is the huge arts complex that houses Amsterdam's Musiektheater, city opera (Stopera) and Town Hall. The colourful stalls of the Waterlooplein Flea Market occupy the space behind the Muziektheater every day except Sunday (see Walk 7). Turn left, walk two blocks along Waterlooplein to Mr Visserplein. Cross this busy junction of four main roads to Mr Visserplein 3 and the Portugees-Israelietische Synagogue.

Although it was built in 1675, this huge red-brick building looks much more modern – perhaps because it was restored in the 1950s. Architect Elias Bouwman is said to have modelled it on the design of the original Temple of Solomon; to some, it looks more prosaically like a warehouse or factory building from the 19th century. Within is one of the world's oldest libraries, along with headquarters of the Dutch rabbinate. The tours of the building are fascinating if you have a real interest in the history and architecture of Amsterdam's Jewish community, but admittedly less gripping if you are merely

a dilettante (the next and final stop on this walk has a greater impact).

PORTUGEES-ISRAELIETISCHE SYNAGOGUE;

SUN-FRI 10-4 www.esnoga.com

8 Turn left out of the synagogue and cross to JD Meierplein, on the south side of Mr Visserplein. The Joods Historisch Museum (Jewish Historical Museum) is at the corner of Jonas Daniel Meierplein and Nieuwe Amstelstraat and is clearly signposted.

Within is the immaculately reconstructed Great Synagogue, possibly the earliest remaining synagogue in Europe. It was built in 1671. The building also contains three other Ashkenazi synagogues: the Obbene Shul (Upper Synagogue), built in 1685; the Dritt Schul (Third Synagogue), which opened in 1700, and the Nieuwe Shul (New Synagogue), built in 1752. All were sacked by the German occupying forces (and their Dutch collaborators) during World War II and have been painstakingly restored. A high point is the marble ark of the Great Synagogue; the exhibition of false papers used by Jews desperate to escape capture by the Nazis strikes a grimmer note. One of the most moving exhibits is the self-painted story of the artist Charlotte Salomon, killed at Auschwitz at the age of 26.

JOODS HISTORISCH MUSEUM;

DAILY 11-5 www.jhm.nl

9 The walk ends here. Retrace your steps to Waterlooplein for the metro, tram or museum boat.

Resistance and Occupation

This walk may leave you in a sombre mood – and perhaps it should. It celebrates the heroes and martyrs of the German occupation of 1940-45.

Amsterdam has a reputation for resistance to oppression. The story of the long struggle against Spain is well known. Less celebrated is the revolt of the Patriot party in 1787 against the oppressive regime of William V. The Patriots were defeated with the help of William's brother in law, Frederick William II of Prussia, but in 1795, with the help of revolutionary France, they formed the Batavian Republic, inspired by the ideals of the French Revolution. By 1804, the Republic had fallen out with France and Napoleon installed his brother Louis as King of Holland. The French finally left in 1813, as Napoleon's empire crumbled. The House of Orange returned in the person of William VI, who was crowned in 1815. Most celebrated of all is the story of Dutch resistance to the five-year German occupation which began in May 1940. Not all Netherlanders resisted the Nazis. Many were active Nazi collaborators. Tens of thousands of Dutchmen volunteered to join the Waffen SS and fight for the Third Reich.

1 Leaving the metro, walk through the cheerful but trashy Waterlooplein market. Keep the huge Muziektheater and Stadhuis-Opera complex (generally called the Stopera) on your left until you reach the water of the Zwanenburgwal.

The Waterlooplein became the main market of the surrounding Jewish quarter in 1886, after the older markets in Jodenbreestraat and St Anthoniesbreestraat were swept away to make way for a broader thoroughfare through the district. Because of the restrictions placed on Jewish traders since the 17th century, they always had to sell their wares on the street. Waterlooplein was named in honour of the famous battle of 1815, in which the Dutch fought on the winning side – by then, Napoleon Bonaparte had made himself thoroughly unpopular in the Netherlands.

In 1985 *kraker* (squatter) demonstrators clashed with police here in a bid to 'Stop the Stopera' – they wanted affordable workers' housing instead. Sadly, the Battle of Waterlooplein was the last stand of Amsterdam's once-potent political counter-culture, signalling an end to three decades of brave hippy resistance to the bourgeoisification of the city.

2 Turn left when you reach the canal and, keeping the water on your right, look out for a black marble monolith slap in the middle of the canalside walkway.

This monument to the Jewish resistance fighters of World War II was erected in 1988. It's largely forgotten that the first group to take up arms against the Germans was the Dutch Communist Party, in which Jewish fighters played a huge part. Few of them survived.

3 Turn left again and with the café-terrace of the Stopera complex on your left and the Amstel on your right, walk along Amstel for around 200yd (183m), towards the Blauwbrug. Just before you reach the bridge, look left and down.

Outlined on the pavement is the ground plan of the Megadle Jethomiem orphanage, founded in 1738 to care for parentless Ashkenazi boys. In March 1943, the children in its care were deported to the Sobibor death camp. It was demolished in 1977 to make way for the Stopera complex.

4 Walk on to the Blauwbrug, cross the street and carry on down the Amstel to the wooden swing-bridge that crosses the Nieuwe Herengracht.

Walter Suskind, for whom the bridge is named, was one of many German Jews who fled to Amsterdam when the Nazis came to power, only to be caught up by the occupation of the Netherlands. An actor and impresario, he was coerced during the occupation to serve on the puppet Joodse Raad (Jewish Council) as the man in charge of its deportation programme. Many Jewish leaders thought co-operating with the occupiers was the only hope for the survival of

51

DISTANCE **1.5 miles (2.4km)**

ALLOW **1.5 hours**

START **Waterlooplein**

FINISH **Plantage Parklaan**

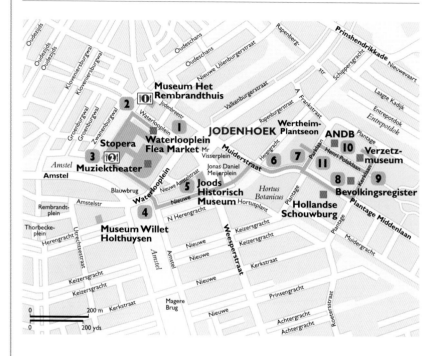

their community. They were wrong: in total 107,000 Dutch Jews were sent to the death camps. Fewer than 5,000 survived. Suskind was not among them – but before he was sent to his death at Auschwitz, he arranged for the escape of almost 1,000 Jewish children who would otherwise have been murdered. His story deserves to be better known.

5 Don't cross the Walter Suskindbrug – instead turn left onto Nieuwe Herengracht. Walk all the way to the other end, cross the busy (and characterless) Weesperstraat, and turn left into Jonas Daniel Meijerplein.

J D Meijer (1780-1834) was the first Jew to become a lawyer in the Netherlands. A campaigner for the rights of his fellow Jews, he was also among the first to suggest that poverty might be one of the causes of crime. In the middle of the square, the bronze Dokwerker (Dock Worker) statue commemorates the workers who declared a general strike

ABOVE: DENKMAL DE DOKWERKERS

on 25 February 1941 in protest against the deportation of Amsterdam's Jews. Unfortunately, the workers' organizations underestimated German ruthlessness and the willingness of the Dutch police to collaborate with the occupiers. The strike was broken within three days, deportation of Jews was carried through, and members of Dutch trade unions joined them on the Nazis' death lists.

6 Return to Nieuwe Herengracht and, with the canal on your right, walk to the corner of J D Meijerplein and turn right to cross Nieuwe Herengracht by the Muiderstraat bridge. Muiderstraat is a dull main road that becomes Plantage Middenlaan. Follow its north side briskly, with the greenery of the Hortus Botanicus on your right and the Wertheim-Plantseon park on your left. At the corner of Plantage Middenlaan and Plantage Parklaan look out for two marble sphinxes flanking the entrance to the Wertheim-Plantseon. Turn left, through the entrance, into the park.

In the centre of this small park is a memorial to the victims of Auschwitz by Dutch sculptor Jan Wolkers. Six shattered mirrors reflect the sky, and the central section is inscribed *'Nooit meer Auschwitz'* ('Auschwitz: never again').

7 Backtrack to the park entrance, cross Plantage Parklaan and cross again to the south side of Plantage Middenlaan and turn left. Midway along the block (about 200yd/183m) is the Hollandse Schouwburg.

Until the German occupation, the Hollandse Schouwburg was a hub of Amsterdam cultural life, and many of its stars and impresarios came from the Jewish community. In 1942 it was commandeered by the Germans as the headquarters of the Joodse Raad's deportation programme. It was from here that Walter Suskind and others helped to spirit away some of the children who were marked for deportation. In 1962 it became an official monument, and is now run as an annex to the Joods Historisch Museum (see Walk 6). Inside, a memorial wall bears 6,700 surnames, which represent more than 104,000 Dutch Jews killed during the occupation.

8 Cross at the first opportunity to the north side of Plantage Middenlaan, turn right, and after half a block take the next left onto Plantage Kerklaan. Keep to the left side of the street. Half a block up, look for No. 36.

This was the Bevolkingsregister (Amsterdam Registry Office). During World War II, its records were used by the Nazis and their collaborators to identify Jews, Communists and trade unionists for deportation. A plaque commemorates the resistance fighters who attacked the building on 27 March 1943 in a bid to burn its files. They failed – the index cards were too tight-packed to burn easily – and 12 of them were shot.

9 Carry on along Plantage Kerklaan for half a block. The next turning on your left is Henri Polaklaan. Cross it, and midway up the next block turn left, up stone steps and through an arched, white stone doorway into No. 61a.

This conspicuous and dignified red-brick building, dating from 1875, housed a number of Jewish musical and dramatic clubs until World War II. Since 1999 it has been the home of the Versetzmuseum (Occupation Museum). This outstandingly brave and candid museum summarizes Dutch resistance to the German occupation, but does not shrink from the uglier facts of Dutch collaboration with the Nazis.

VERSETZMUSEUM;

TUE-FRI 10-5, SAT-SUN 12-5

www.versetzmuseum.org

10 Leaving the Occupation Museum turn right, walk back down to Henri Polaklaan and turn right again. At the end of the block, at No. 9, is the ANDB building.

As John Lennon sang, 'a working class hero is something to be'. Henri Polak (1868-1943) was one: the first chairman of the Algemeene Nederlandse Diamantbewerkers Bond (Dutch Diamond Workers Union), which he helped to create in 1894. The ANDB was the first trade union in the world to win an eight-hour working day for its members, and the first in the Netherlands to win the right to an annual holiday for the workers. Polak also helped to set up the Nederlands Verbond van Vakverenigingen (Dutch Trade Unions Congress) and the Dutch Social-

WHERE TO EAT

10 CAFÉ DE SLUYSWACHT,
Jodenbreestraat 1;
Tel: 020 625 7611.
www.sluyswacht.nl
Pleasant, light café with canalside terrace, serving drinks and a good choice of salads and snacks. €€

10 CAFÉ DANTZIG,
Zwanenbrugwal 15;
Tel: 020 620 9039.
Big, lively café which is part of the Stopera complex. Excellent open-air terrace looking over the Amstel and wide menu of international light meals and snacks. €€

Democratic Workers Party. As a Jew, a socialist and a trade unionist, he was one of the first to be arrested by the Nazis in 1940. Ill-treated while imprisoned, he died in 1943. The ANDB's former headquarters is now the Nationaal Vakbondsmuseum (National Trade Unions Museum) – probably the only museum in the world that portrays trade unions and their achievements in resisting exploitation and oppression in a positive light. From the start of the German occupation, the trade union movement formed a powerful basis for resistance.

11 Leaving the museum cross to the opposite side of Plantage Parklaan. Tram 6 southbound takes you back to Plantage Kerklaan. Change here for tram 3 or 9 to return to the city centre.

Museumplein and the Great Gallery Crawl

Amsterdam's awesome art collections cluster around Museumplein. Be prepared to queue to visit the Rijksmuseum and the Van Gogh Museum.

Museumplein is separated from the old city centre by the Singelgracht, the outermost of Amsterdam's concentric canal rings. Here, three museums just a few steps apart from each other celebrate quite different schools of art. The Rijksmuseum's collection focuses on the classic works of the old masters – Rembrandt, Hals, Vermeer, the Breughels and many more – and their antecedents and successors. The Van Gogh Museum pays a belated posthumous tribute to the work of mad, sad, brilliant Vincent. And the Stedelijk worships at the altar of op, pop, abstract and post-modern art. These three great collections are housed in buildings that are works of art in their own right and reflect their contents. Such a concentration of artistic genius can be overwhelming. Fortunately, Amsterdam's biggest green space, the Vondelpark, is at hand. At its best in summer, it allows you room to stretch your legs, take a deep breath and mull over what you have just seen.

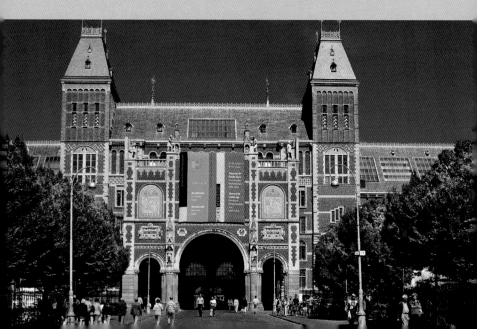

Leave the café-cluttered Leidseplein from its south corner and follow Weteringschans (with the prominent Holland Casino complex on your right) along the Singelgracht for one block. You'll spot the Rijksmuseum some distance off. Cross the Singelgracht by the first bridge you come to, cross Stadhouderskade, and walk around the building to the entrance to the Philips Wing, at the rear of the building.

This Dutch neo-Renaissance, red-brick pile should (if you've been paying attention to your surroundings) remind you of another grandiose, 19th-century Amsterdam landmark. Yes, the Rijksmuseum is unmistakably the work of P J H Cuypers, architect of Centraal Station and not a man to skimp on his façades. When it opened in 1885 it caused much tutting and talk of public money wasted on art that could have been better spent elsewhere. Now, of course,

it's regarded as *the* jewel in Amsterdam's tourism crown, and an open cheque has been written for its refurbishment, which should be complete by 2013. Cuypers's ghost must be feeling smug.

Unfortunately, this means that most of the Rijksmuseum's huge treasury of art (more than 5,000 paintings, one million prints, sketches and etchings, and thousands of sculptures and other works) is inaccessible. But the top stuff is still on show in the redesigned Philips Wing, which includes the one painting everyone comes to see: Rembrandt's huge, vigorous and best-known work: *The Guard Company of Captain Frans Banning Cocq and Lieutenant Willem van Ruijtenburc*, better known as *The Night Watch* (painted between 1640 and 1642). The name is misleading: the jolly band of arquebusiers are painted suited, booted, locked and loaded in broad daylight. This is no stiff, set-piece portrait – it almost looks like a frame from a graphic novel. Until restoration of the main museum is complete, the Philips Wing also shows around 400 of the Rijksmuseum's most important works. Many of these are drawn from the private collection of Stadhouder (Prince) William V (1748-1806), bequeathed to the nation after his death and embellished by further gifts from patriotic patrons of the arts, including works by Jan Steen (1626-79), Johannes Vermeer (1632-75) and Frans Hals (1580-1666) as well as a selection from the museum's wonderful portfolio of Rembrandts.

RIJKSMUSEUM;

SUN-THU 9-6, FRI 9-10 www.rijksmuseum.nl

DISTANCE **2.5 miles (4km)**

ALLOW **4-5 hours**

START **Leidseplein**

FINISH **Leidseplein**

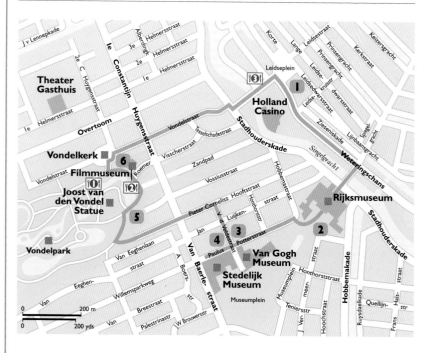

2 Leaving the Rijksmuseum behind you, cut across the open space of the Museumplein to Paulus Potterstraat. Don't cross the road. Turn left and walk one short block down to the Van Gogh Museum. Pick up a coffee from the stand next to the museum to drink while you queue to enter. To get the most out of your visit, start with the introductory exhibition on the ground floor, then work your way through the permanent collection on the first floor to the Print Room, also on the first floor.

Rembrandt may have gone bust, but at least he had his time in the sun. Poor Vincent van Gogh (1853–90) sold just one painting in his lifetime, so his depression and subsequent suicide at the age of 37 are not surprising. The sheer intensity of his work has to be seen to be believed. The collection here is laid out chronologically, starting with the earthier realism of earlier works such *The Potato Eaters* (1885), leading to the vivid colours and swashing brush strokes of paintings inspired by the blazing sun of Provence.

Despite the support of his younger brother Theo, a prosperous Amsterdam art dealer, van Gogh became increasingly desperate and depressed during his time in Provence. After mutilating himself by severing the lobe of his left ear (which he offered to a local prostitute named Rachel, asking her to keep it safe – we can only imagine her reaction), he committed himself to an asylum at St-Remy. The looming skies and tormented trees of his last works, such as *Wheatfield with Crows*, hint at his final despair.

The museum has 200 of van Gogh's paintings and 500 of his drawings, along with his personal collection of marvellous Japanese prints – it's immediately obvious that the colours and swirling movement of Japanese artists were a huge influence on his work.

It also has an array of works by Gauguin (1848–1903), Monet (1840–1926), and Pissarro (1830–1903). It was Gauguin who inspired van Gogh to move to Provence, where they painted together – a friendship immortalized in the 1956 film *Lust for Life* (an ironic title if ever there was one), starring Kirk Douglas as Vincent and Anthony Quinn as Gauguin.

VAN GOGH MUSEUM;

SUN-THU 9-6, FRI 9-10

www.vangoghmuseum.nl

3 Go back out the way you came in, turn left on Paulus Potterstraat and cross Van der Veldestraat. The Stedelijk (Municipal) Museum occupies the whole of the block and the entrance is midway down. Closed for refurbishment while this book was being researched, it is due

to reopen in mid-2009. If it hasn't reopened by the time of your visit, proceed to (4).

This museum's dull name and its staid 19th-century exterior belie its contents. Its collection embraces pop-art pioneers such as Roy Lichtenstein and Andy Warhol, as well as Jackson Pollock, Kandinsky, Chagall, Monet, Picasso, Cezanne and the Dutch painters Piet Mondriaan and Theo van Doesberg, founders of the *Stijl* movement in art and design. They're all wimps when compared with Kazimir Malevich, founder of the Suprematist school, who aimed to reduce art to 'the supremacy of pure feeling' through geometric abstraction. Seek out his *Self Portrait in Two Dimensions* – a self portrait unlike any other, since it's a

59

WHERE TO EAT

[O] 'T BLAUE THEEHUIS,
Vondelpark 5;
Tel: 020 662 0254.
www.blauwetheehuis.nl
This Vondelpark landmark is the
perfect place for lunch or afternoon
tea at the end of this walk. €€

[O] CAFE VERTIGO,
Vondelpark 3;
Tel: 020 612 3021.
www.nederlandsfilmmuseum.nl
The Film Museum's café-restaurant
is cosy in winter and has a pleasant
terrace for better weather. €

[O] CAFÉ AMERICAIN,
Leidseplein 26;
Tel: 020 556 3232.
Artists, writers and bohemians are
said to have frequented this Art-Deco
café since it opened in 1902. €€€

Cornelisz Hoofstraat. Walk one block to
the entrance to the Vondelpark. Carry
on along the footpath that is an
extension of P C Hoofstraat. Take the
first right, towards the lake and the
statue of Joost van den Vondel.

This 120-acre (48ha) rectangle of lawns,
lakes and shrubberies is Amsterdam's
equivalent of London's Hyde Park or
New York's Central Park, and is named
after Joost van den Vondel (1587-1679),
who is to Dutch drama and poetry
what Shakespeare is to English literature.
Landscaped in the late 19th century, on
a sunny summer's day it is busy with

composition of solid-coloured rectangles
and quadrilaterals on a neutral ground.
Born in Kiev of Polish descent, he was
unable to leave the Soviet Union after
the 1918 Revolution and died there in
1935 aged 48. When he fell foul of the
Stalinist regime in the late 1920s, many
of his paintings were smuggled out of the
USSR, not to re-surface until the 1990s.

4 Exit the museum, cross Paulus
Potterstraat, continue along the left
side of Van de Veldestraat, cross Jan
Luijkenstraat and turn left on Pieter

picnickers, amateur musicians and street entertainers. In the hippy summers of the late 1960s and early 1970s it was a virtually self-governing counter-culture commune, until the dream turned sour. But bits of the dream remain, with free open-air rock concerts in summer and a contingent of weekend vendors peddling jewellery and scarves like their hippy grandparents wore 40 years ago.

5 Reach the lake, turn right and keep the lake on your left. Cross Roemer Visscherstraat. Immediately on your right is the 19th-century pavilion which houses the Nederlands Filmmuseum.

The Filmmuseum presents three screenings daily of modern and classic art-house films, in the nostalgic setting of Amsterdam's first picture palace.
FILMMUSEUM; DAILY www.filmmuseum.nl

6 Leave the park by the Filmmuseum Gate. Ahead is the Vondelkerk, designed in the 1870s by P J H Cuypers and named for the poet. Turn right here and follow Vondelstraat for two blocks, crossing Constantijn Huygenstraat and Stadhouderskade, and cross the Singelgracht to find yourself back on Leidseplein where you can pick up trams 1, 2, 5, 6, 7 and 10.

ABOVE: WOODEN FLOORS AND MODERN ART IN THE STEDELIJK MUSEUM

Tiptoe through the Tulips

Experience Tulip Fever at the Tulip Museum then walk across town to see them in bloom – in spring only, of course – at the Hortus Botanic Garden.

The Dutch became obsessed with tulips as early as the mid-16th century, when the first bulbs and flowers were brought to the Netherlands from Turkey, where they had been cultivated for centuries. Constantinople, like Amsterdam, had become home to a Jewish diaspora from Spain and Portugal, so it seems likely that the first tulips arrived by way of Sephardic trade networks. They soon became a national mania. At the time, Amsterdam was the fastest-growing city in Europe. Building space had to be created by dredging land and creating canals, land was at a premium, and only the very wealthiest could afford space for even a tiny garden. And so flowers in pots and window boxes have always been treasured in this intensely built-up city – as has any vestige of greenery. Amsterdam's bigger public green spaces are not found in the historic centre but on its outskirts. Happily, for residents and visitors, the city is so compact that anyone in need of a breath of fresh air need not walk very far to find it.

1 Take tram 13, 14 or 17 to reach Westermarkt. Walk west on Westermarkt, with the unmistakeable landmark of the Westerkerk (see Walk 3) on your right. When you reach Prinsengracht, turn right. Cross Leliegracht where this smaller canal meets Prinsengracht; turn left, cross the bridge over the water of Prinsengracht. Cross the street to Prinsengracht 112, at the corner of Prinsengracht and Egelantiersgracht, the Amsterdam Tulip Museum.

Who would have thought a simple bulb could cause so much trouble? Think of tulips and you think of Amsterdam, but they'd been grown in Central Asia for centuries before they got here – even the name is Turkish. It means 'turban flower'. It took the Dutch and their obsessive genetic tinkering to create the hundreds of flamboyant varieties that exist today. Tulip Fever reached its giddiest heights in the mid-1630s, when speculators poured millions into ever newer and more spectacular varieties. Just one rare bulb could fetch the equivalent of a £1,000 – more than a lifetime's earnings for an ordinary worker. Lots of investors went bust, but the flower continued to fascinate – in 1850 Alexandre Dumas (more famous for *The Three Musketeers*) penned *La Tulipe Noire* (*The Black Tulip*) about the search for a priceless black bloom. A truly black flower is still the Holy Grail for tulip growers.

AMSTERDAM TULIP MUSEUM;

TUE-SUN 10-6

www.amsterdamtulipmuseum.com

2 Exit the museum, cross the street and turn right along Prinsengracht. Cross Bloemgracht, walk past Bloemstraat and at Rozengracht turn left and cross Prinsengracht again. The Westerkerk looms on your left. You are now on the broad Raadhuisstraat. Follow it for three blocks, crossing the Keizersgracht and Herengracht canals. When you reach the Singel, do not cross the water, but turn right and walk along the canal-side with the water on your left until you reach Koningsplein. The famous floating Bloemenmarkt occupies the quayside for the next block.

The Bloemenmarkt is a pale shadow of its former self, but it's still fun. During the 17th and 18th centuries, Amsterdam's canals were crammed with floating markets selling produce from the nearby farmlands and fishing harbours. Several were dedicated to tulips. Today around a dozen stalls, on permanently moored pontoons, offer an incredible choice of seeds, flowers, pot-plants and bulbs, including some wonderfully exotic tulips such as the Black Parrot – a deep purple bloom that is as close as bulb-growers have got to creating a genuine black tulip.

3 Stroll on past the floating flower shops and their pavement displays until you reach Vijzelstraat. Cross this busy main street and dive into Amstelstraat, a scruffy narrow street that leads you after one short block to the north side of touristy Rembrandtplein. Carry on for three very short blocks to the Amstel, which at this

63

DISTANCE 4 miles (6.4km)

ALLOW All day (allowing half a day at the Artis Zoo)

START Westermarkt

FINISH Artis Zoo/Plantage Kerklaan

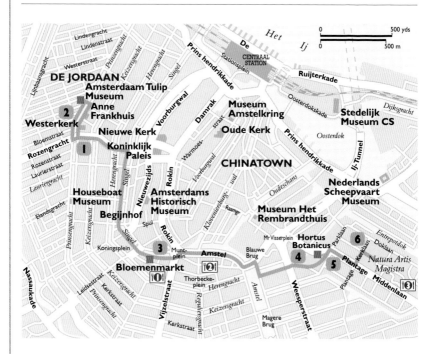

point is recognizably a river, not a narrow canal. Walk straight on, crossing the Blauwe Brug. At the other end, turn right, cross Nieuwe Herengracht by the Walter Suskindbrug drawbridge, then turn left. At the end of the block, cross a busy main road, Weesperstraat, and enter Hortus Plantage.

In the 17th and 18th centuries, city-dwelling Amsterdammers seeking a bit of garden in which to grow flowers and vegetables used to rent small patches of land here, in the district that came to be known as the Plantage. Teahouses and coffee-shops were opened to cater to weekend visitors, and the district came to be known as Amsterdam's pleasure garden. In the 19th century, wealthier citizens seeking more space than the city centre could offer, bought land and built substantial garden villas here.

4 Cross to the north side of the street (your left) and enter the Hortus Botanicus.

OPPOSITE: TULIPS FOR SALE IN THE FLOWER MARKET

Some of the earliest varieties of tulip to be brought to the west can be seen blooming in this historic garden in spring – and it has to be said that they look a bit weedy compared with the varieties that Dutch tulip fanciers managed to produce in later years.

But Amsterdam was interested in the scientific applications of horticulture as well as its aesthetic aspects. Created in 1682, these botanical gardens were sponsored by (among others) the Dutch East India Company as a research centre where Amsterdam's doctors and apothecaries could grow and study the effects – and profitable commercial applications – of plants introduced from Asia, Africa and the Americas, such as coffee, cinnamon, palm oil and pineapple. The medicinal herb garden takes you back to a time when herbal medicines were the only medicines; at the other end of the scientific scale are the high-tech tropical greenhouses that keep steamy jungle plants flourishing even during a Dutch winter.

5 Leave the Hortus Botanicus by its northeast gate, at the corner of Plantage Parklaan and Plantage Middenlaan. Cross to the north side of Plantage Middenlaan, turn right, and walk one block to Plantage Kerklaan. Cross the street, turn left and, halfway up the block, turn right into the Natura Artis Magistra, also known as the Artis Royal Zoo Amsterdam.

Celebrating its 170th anniversary in 2008, this is much more than just a zoo. When it was founded it was unique; it was, in fact, the first zoological garden that was more than just a place for curious people to gawk at exotic creatures. It had its own laboratories, scientific collections and natural history library. This eclectic approach continues, with the opening of a Geological Museum in 1992 and a Planetarium in 1998 and (both are included in the price of admission).

From late January until the end of May, the Artis is probably the best place to tiptoe through the tulips in Amsterdam, with thousands of bulbs in bloom – daffodils, crocuses and alpine exotics as well as tulips. For the rest of the year, more exotics flourish in the hothouses to the rear of the zoo. Next to the outdoor chimp enclosure is the oldest tree in Amsterdam, a 250-year-old oak, and in the Japanese Stone Garden two venerable gingko trees flank a green bronze image of the Buddha.

You could spend all day here, but if your time is limited you should follow the zoo's Highlights Route, which takes you to the gibbon island, the small mammal house, the elephant enclosure, wolf wood, the aquarium, penguin rock, the sea lion pool, the polar bears, the creepie-crawlie insect house, giraffes and antelopes in the African Savannah section, and a new South American section with giant anteaters, capybaras

and maned wolves. Artis is also dotted with more than 50 sculptures, some of them dating from the early years of the Dutch Royal Zoological Society, others much more recent – including a powerful collection of Tengenenge carvings from contemporary Zimbabwe.

ARTIS ROYAL ZOO;
DAILY 9-5 www.artis.nl

6 From the Plantage Kerklaan exit, tram 6, 9, 10 or 14 will take you back to the city centre. However, it's more fun to take the *Artis Expres* canal boat back to Centraal Station: tickets are sold at the zoo entrance/exit and the boat stop is clearly signposted.

WHERE TO EAT

🍴 RESTAURANT SELECTA,
Vijzelstraat 26;
Tel: 020 624 8894.
www.restaurantselecta.nl
Authentic Indonesian cooking close to the Bloemenmarkt. €€

🍴 DE KROON,
Rembrandtplein 17;
Tel: 020 625 2011.
www.dekroon.nl
Handy halfway point. €€€

🍴 DE TWEE CHEETAHS,
Artis Zoo;
Tel: 020 624 5522.
www.artis.nl
Watch cheeky meerkats and other fauna while you dine. €€

TULIP BULB STALL IN THE FLOATING FLOWER MARKET

Rioting Workers and Bohemians in Jordaan

Keep looking upwards for clues to the former residents of this district – you'll find them in the building's decorative gable stones.

Jordaan is bounded by the Prinsengracht, Brouwersgracht, Lijnbaansgracht and Looiersgracht canals. Street names like Lindengracht and Anjeliersgracht are reminders of the maze of small canals (*grachts*) that were little more than ditches dug to drain the swampy land. Until the Golden Age, this area housed smellier businesses – such as breweries and tanneries – that weren't welcome in the posher parts of the city, along with the slums that housed their workers. Later, the Jordaan's streets of higgledy-piggledy houses became home to less-well-off merchants and shopkeepers, workers and exiles like the Huguenots, and it had a bit of a reputation as a tough working-class area where the law feared to tread. Workers, angered by lay-offs, pay cuts and rising prices, rioted here in the 1930s, and urban renewal began only after World War II. In the 1960s – like London's Chelsea or Soho – the Jordaan became the trendy spot for young bohemians, but despite gentrification it still keeps more than a whiff of its original character, with the finest portfolio of tobacco-tinted 'brown cafes' in the city.

1 Take the tram or metro to Centraal Station. Leave Stationsplein by whichever bridge is handiest: cross the Open Haven, cross Prins Hendrikkade and turn right. At Martelaarsgracht, cross, turn left and carry on walking for two short blocks to Hekelsveld, at the north end of Spuistraat. Turn right here onto Kattengat.

On the left side of Kattengat, look up to the step gables of the houses at No. 4–6. These still bear the names *De Gouden Spiegel* and *De Silveren Spiegel* – the Golden Mirror and the Silver Mirror. Built in 1614 for a wealthy soap manufacturer, the names are a play on the owner's name: Laurens Jansz Spiegel.

2 Turn right into Stromarkt and look out for some more architectural puns above the doors of some of the attractive restored 17th-century houses.

A salmon carved above the door of No. 37 reminds us that the original owners were the Salm family – *salm* is Dutch for salmon. The bear peeking out from a stone castle on the gable of No. 9 is another pun: this was the home of Hendrik Beerenburg, whose surname translates as 'Bearcastle'. Above the door is a carved winged lion of St Mark, holding a bible open with its paw. This is the symbol of Venice, so Beerenburg may have had some Venetian connection.

3 Continue along the Stromarkt to reach the Singel; turn right, then almost immediately left across the Haarlemmersluis bridge, left again then first right onto the Brouwersgracht. Carry on along Brouwersgracht for two blocks, crossing the Herengracht and Keizersgracht where they join Brouwersgracht, until you reach Prinsengracht. Turn left across the Papiermoelensluis bridge to the east (odd-numbered) side of Prinsengracht.

Look up at the gablestones of the houses on your left, just after the bridge, which depict biblical scenes. At No. 1a stands St Peter, with a fish in his left hand. At No. 3 are two wanderers from Emmaus to whom Jesus appeared after the Resurrection, and at No. 5 is a distinctly militant-looking St Paul, with a bible in one hand and a sword in the other.

71

DISTANCE **4 miles (6.4km)**

ALLOW **3 hours**

START **Stationsplein**

FINISH **Westermarkt**

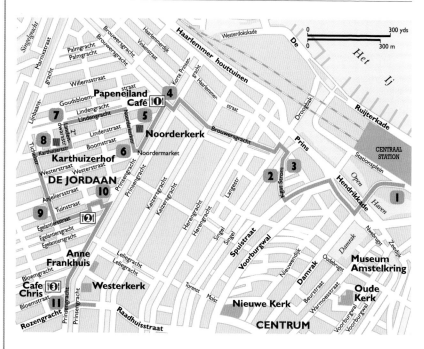

4 Now cross the Prinsegracht by the Lekkeresluis bridge.

Right in front of you at the corner of the two canals is the Papeneiland Café, one of the oldest 'brown cafés' in Amsterdam. The Papeneiland (Papists's Island) gets its name from the Carthusian monastery that stood here until the Reformation, while the Lekkersluis (Sweet Bridge) is named for the pancake sellers who once hawked their wares here. You can still get a good pancake in the café.

5 Coming out of the café, turn right down Prinsengracht, with the hulking Noorderkerk on your right. Past the church, turn right into the Noordermarkt.

Look up at the decorative gablestones along the north side of the square. *Vrouwe Fortuna* (Dame Fortune) stands above No.16, flanked by rolls of cloth, chests and cash-boxes. A ship decorates No. 17, so it's a good guess that both houses were owned by merchant captains.

Jordaaners seem to have been ready to riot at the drop of a hat. In this street on 25 July 1886, the pretext was an eel-pulling contest – a popular local pastime involving a live eel coated with soap to make it even more slippery. An interfering policeman tried to stop the event. The crowd objected and locked him up. When fellow-officers tried to free him, they were bombarded with cobbles, roof-tiles and flower pots. The army was called in, and in three days of street fighting 26 people were killed. Community policing has come a long way since then.

Landlubbers lived at No. 18 (a sheep), No. 19 (a chicken) and No. 21 (a cow). In the 16th and 17th centuries this was Amsterdam's main livestock market. You won't find cattle or sheep here any more, but on a Saturday, when the Boerenmarkt (Farmers' Market) is in full swing, you'll still see chickens (mostly fancy breeds), pigeons, parrots and tropical finches, while locals queue to buy farm produce.

6 From the north side of the square, turn right on Noorderkerkstraat, then left on Lindengracht.

Walking along the odd-numbered side of this street, look out for the fanciful gablestone at No. 57. This shows 'the world turned upside down', with fish roosting in trees, the year of the building's construction inverted, and the inscription *T Hcargnednil* – which is Lindengracht spelt backwards.

7 Turn left on Tweede Lindendwarsstraat, then right onto Karthuizerstraat. On the right, at No. 89, is the Karthuizerhof.

This almshouse, built in 1650 on land formerly owned by the Carthusian monastery that stood nearby from 1392 until the end of the 16th century, has one of the largest courtyards in Amsterdam. In the inner courtyard stands a brick pump-house with two fanciful sea-monster spouts, and the walls bear the three diagonal crosses that are Amsterdam's city coat of arms, and the merchant ship that is another of the city's symbols.

8 Turn left out of the courtyard, walk to the end of Karthuizerstraat and left on Tichelstraat. Ahead of you is the grandiose spire of the Westerkerk, a few blocks away on the other side of Prinsengracht. Cross Westerstraat and then carry on into Tweede

Anjeliersdwarstraat. This is the Jordaan's coolest eating and shopping area, packed with cafés, bars, boutiques and galleries.

Like London's Chelsea, this part of town was at its hippest in the 1960s, when creative young bohemians moved in. It's moved up-market since then, but there's still a whiff of nostalgic bohemianism.

9 This thoroughfare changes its name block by block. After less than 100yd (91m), at the end of the first block, it becomes Tweede Tuindwarstraat, then the Tweede Egelantiersdwarstraat (dwarstraat means 'cross street'). At the end of Tweede Egelantiersdwarstraat, turn left into Egelantiersstraat, then left again at Eerste Egelantiersdwarstraat.

On your right, a wooden door set into a plain stone wall leads into the three quiet courtyards of the Claes Claeszoon Hofje, another of the Jordaan's historic almshouses. It's now part of the Sweelinck Conservatory.

10 Walk through the courtyards to the small alley that brings you back onto Egelantiersstraat; turn left, and walk less than 100yd (91m) to the Prinsengracht. Turn right, and follow the west side of Prinsengracht to the junction with the Bloemgracht. On Bloemgracht is another venerable tavern.

Lots of 'brown cafés' claim to be the oldest in town. Café Chris's claim is stronger than most: there's firm

WHERE TO EAT

IOI CAFÉ PAPENEILAND,
Prinsengracht 2;
Tel: 020 624 1989.
Atmospheric and cosy, in a prime location next to a scenic canal. €

IOI CAFÉ 'T SMALLE,
Egelantiersgracht 12;
Tel: 020 344 4560.
Built in 1786, this was the tasting house for the famous Pieter Hope gin distillery. Restored in the 1970s; serves drinks and light meals. €

IOI CAFÉ CHRIS,
Bloemstraat 42;
Tel 020 624 5942.
www.cafechris.nl
Another claimant for the 'oldest café in Amsterdam' title, serving drinks and snacks just across the canal from the Westerkerk. €

documentary evidence that there has been a tavern here since 1624, and the masons working on the Westerkerk were paid their weekly wages here.

11 Walk two very short blocks to Rozengracht and the bridge that crosses over the Prinsengracht to the Westerkerk – there's a great view of the spire from this side of the canal. From here, a 5-10 minute walk brings you back to the Dam, from where you have a choice of trams 13, 14 and 17 at the Westermarkt.

CAFÉ CHRIS, ONE OF THE CITY'S 'BROWN CAFES'

A Walk on the Seamy Side

This walk is not for the strait-laced, but it does offer a glimpse into Amsterdam's underside, and provides more than a little food for thought.

Amsterdam's approach to the sex industry is pragmatic: you can't stop it, so you might as well live with it, license it, tax it and make sure people are well informed about the risks. The Oudezijd (Old Side) is a narrow rectangle of land between the Oudezijds Voorburgwal (Within the Town Wall) and Oudezijds Achterburgwal (Outside the Town Wall) canals. At its northern end, the fleshpots of the Rosse Buurt (Red Light district), with windows from which near-naked or fetishistically clad sex workers beckon, spill over to either side of Oudezijds Voorburgwal – overlooked by two of the city's landmark churches. Interspersed with the brothels, massage parlours, sex shops and go-go bars are ordinary stores and homes; it's not unusual to see a little old lady calmly doing her grocery shopping next to a statuesque leather-clad transvestite. In daylight, it all looks pretty shabby, but after dark the glow of neon bar signs lends it a spurious glamour. Violent crime is fairly rare, but pickpockets and bag snatchers are common. At night, avoid poorly lit alleys, and do not photograph sex workers.

Leave Centraal Station from its main entrance. Cross Stationsplein and follow Damrak over the wide bridge that crosses the Open Haven. Continue over the bridge, cross Prins Hendrikkade, and continue down the east side of Damrak to No. 18 on your right.

The Amsterdam Sex Museum, aka the Venustempel, claims to be the world's first and oldest sex museum. It opened in 1985. Its collection has been gathered personally by the owners and now covers four floors, attracting around half a million visitors a year and inspiring imitators around the world. Inside, you can see objects and erotica illustrating sexual attitudes spanning some 4,000 years of human history – shocking, eye-opening or a bit dull, depending on how you feel about such things. Don't miss the 7ft (2.1m) high penis chairs!

SEX MUSEUM;
DAILY www.sexmuseumamsterdam.nl

2 Walk on down Damrak to Oude Brugsteeg; cross Damrak, and walk along with the water of the Damrak on your left to Warmoesstraat. This is the oldest street in the city and has seen better days. Cross it, turn right, and walk down to No. 141, next to the corner of Warmoesstraat and St Annenstraat.

'Sometimes the safe-sex message can be brought across better with a smile', say the founders of Condomerie Het Gulden Vlies, founded in 1987, and you'd have to be very prudish indeed not to be amused

WHERE TO EAT

[O] CAFÉ ROUX,
Oudezijds Voorburgwal 197;
Tel: 020 555 3560.
Posh brasserie of the Hotel Grand Amsterdam, overlooking the canal and with a traditional French menu inspired by the legendary French chef Albert Roux. €€€

[O] IN 'T AEPJEN,
Zeedik 1;
Tel: 020 626 8401.
Located in one of the oldest buildings in Amsterdam, this eccentrically decorated bar was once a sailors' flophouse. Its name – the Little Ape – harks back to the days when sailors made extra money by bringing monkeys back from their travels to sell as pets (the author's grandfather used to do this). €

– and informed – by their thriving business-cum-information centre, where you can buy condoms in every conceivable hue, texture and flavour. And, yes, it seems that size does matter.

Find out about the history of the condom, going all the way back to the days of the infamous Casanova and Dr Johnson's sidekick Boswell, who forgot to bring any with him when he visited Amsterdam in the 18th century, and consequently had to forgo one of his favourite pastimes.

CONDOMERIE HET GULDEN VLIES;
MON-SAT 11-6 www.condomerie.com

DISTANCE **1 mile (1.6km)**

ALLOW **1 hour**

START **Stationsplein**

FINISH **Damrak**

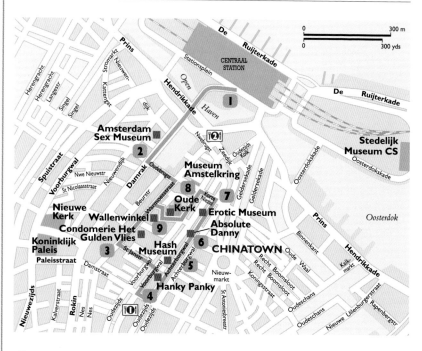

3 Turn left out of the condom shop and at the next corner, turn left on St Janstraat. Walk about 100yd (91m) to Oudezijds Voorburgwal; cross the canal, and turn right. About 50yd (46m) down, at No. 141, is what claims to be the most famous tattoo shop in the world.

Hanky Panky Tattooing has been leaving its indelible mark on international stars and celebs since 1979. Tattoo king Henk Schiffmacher's client list reads like a roll-call of rock'n' roll royalty (recent clients include former Spice Girl Mel C and supermodel Kate Moss). The Hanky Panky crew will tattoo anything you want, anywhere you want it. Even if you decide against acquiring an outlandish body embellishment that you may well have to live with forever while you're here, the illustrations of satisfied clients are eye-opening examples of what people will do to achieve individuality.

HANKY PANKY TATTOOING;

DAILY 11-8 www.hankypankysthehangout.com

4 Exiting the shop, turn left and with the canal on your right, walk down less than 50yd (46m) to Oude Doelenstraat. Turn left, and follow this very short street to Oudezijds Achterburgwal. Do not cross the canal. Turn left and walk up one block. Cross St Janstraat, and at the corner, enter No. 130 Oudezijds Achterburgwal.

The Hash Marijuana Hemp Museum has been making the case for cannabis since 1985. In summer 2008 it moved into a new building, with a slick presentation of its multifarious and multicultural exhibits. This is far more than just a stoner's paradise. It sells seeds of some of the most powerful strains that the twisted minds of Dutch alternative horticulturalists have been able to create – along with pot paraphernalia such as the patent Vaporizer (which eliminates the need to fill your lungs with harmful smoke) and an array of bongs, chillums and rolling papers. But as well as celebrating the recreational and medicinal uses of *Cannabis indica*, it highlights the 'killer weed' as a valuable source of fuel, fibre, construction materials and foodstuffs. If the museum doesn't make you at least question the extent to which the stuff is demonized in some countries, your thinking must be very rigid indeed.

HASH MARIJUANA HEMP MUSEUM;
DAILY 10-10 www.hashmuseum.com

5 With the canal still on your right, walk on up Oudezijds Achterburgwal to the Oudekennissteeg bridge. Just before the bridge, at No. 78

81

Oudezijds Achterburgwal, is Absolute Danny. Depending on your tastes and your sense of adventure, either pop inside or avert your eyes and walk briskly past…

Scary lady Danny Linden's shop celebrates tight-fitting rubber garments and sells all the latest equipment to accessorize them. And we are not talking scuba kit. Should you wish to try out your purchases in discreetly equipped comfort, Danny even has her own hotel – check out www.absolutesuite.com. The Marquis de Sade would have loved it.

ABSOLUTE DANNY;
SUN-THU 11-9, FRI-SAT 11-10
www.absolutedanny.com

6 Calm down, cross Oudekennissteeg, and on your left at No. 54 Oudezijds Achterburgwal is the Erotic Museum.

If Danny's latex paradise turned you on, the Erotic Museum is quite likely to turn you right off again. Like the rival Sex Museum, it tries rather too hard and the result is clinical, bordering on infantile. A jumble of exhibits covers five floors and includes some childishly naughty drawings by John Lennon (worth a fortune, presumably, but not outstanding art), a collection of sex-toys through the ages, and a floor of fairly repellent hard-core pornographic videos. It may all have been very daring and cutting edge when the museum first opened, but in the 21st century it all just seems a bit sad and grubbily predictable.

7 Exit the museum onto Oudezijds Achterburgwal, turn left, and walk up to the next corner. Turn left on Korte Niezel, and return to Oudezijds Voorburgwal. Cross the canal, turn left, and then immediately right onto Oudekerksplein – the landmark of the Oude Kerk, Amsterdam's oldest place of worship, is unmissable.

On Oudekerksplein, a new bronze statue (erected in 2007) is the work of sculptor Els Rijense. It is dedicated to women and men who work in the sex industry around the world.

8 Walk round Oudekerksplein to reach the corner of Engekerksteeg, and at No. 3 find Wallenwinkel (the Red Light District Store).

Run by the Prostitution Information Centre (PIC), Wallenwinkel was founded by ex-prostitute Mariska Majoor in 1994 to promote the decriminalization of prostitution. The PIC's argument is that if someone chooses freely to work as a prostitute and is able to work responsibly and in clean and healthy conditions then there is no reason why they should not do so – a refreshingly honest and upfront approach to the subject.

PIC;
TUE-SAT 12-7 www.pic-amsterdam.nl

9 Engekerksteeg leads in less than 25yd (23m) back to Warmoesstraat. Turn right here, then left, to find yourself back on Damraak, within sight of Centraal Station.

AMSTERDAM'S RED LIGHT DISTRICT

Bridges and Beer on the Amstel

Amsterdam once had hundreds of small independent breweries. Now there are very few left – this walk starts in one and ends in another.

Most of Amsterdam's old breweries produced a range of beers, from thirst-quenching light ales to potent winter warmers, and most had their own tavern or *proeflokaal*, where customers could sample the product before buying. Many also made Amsterdam's favourite spirit, *geniever*. In any 'brown café' you can still ask for a *borrel*, a *pikketanussie*, a *hassiebassie*, a *keiltje* or a *slokkie*, and what you will get is shot of something very much like gin, only more so – distilled from grain or potatoes and flavoured with juniper and other herbs. If you want to show off, ask for a *kamelenkrug* (camel's hump) – a glass so full that you can't lift it without spilling. Instead, lower your lips to the glass for that first sip. For a beer chaser, ask for a *lampie licht* (little lamp), a *bakkie* (jar) or a *kopstoot* (knock on the head). Amsterdam's two brewing giants, Heineken and Amstel, merged some years ago and moved their premises from the banks of the Amstel to a giant new plant outside the city, and the former Heineken brewery has been transformed into a purpose-built visitor attraction and merchandizing operation.

1 Take the metro to Nieuwmarkt. Leave Nieuwmarkt from its southwest corner and walk just a few yards down Kloveniersburgwal to No. 6.

De Bekeerde Suster (The Converted Sister) stands on a site where nuns from a nearby convent began brewing beer (for medicinal purposes only, of course) as early as 1544. Today, one of Amsterdam's small independent companies, Beeiardgroep, has a microbrewery on the premises. Visit around midday for a behind-the-scenes tour of the gleaming copper and stainless-steel vats, or just drop in to sample a glass of their Blonde Ros, Bock Ros or Winter Ros beer.

DE BEKEERDE SUSTER;

WED-THU 12 noon; reservations required for brewery visit and beer-tasting. TEL: 020 423 0112. www.beiaardgroup.nl

2 This walk is just beginning, so don't over-indulge. Carry on down Kloveniersburgwal for five blocks, to the very end, and bear right on Nieuwe Doelenstraat. You're now passing through the heart of the city's University quarter, with the campus and library buildings of the university and the buildings of the Theatre School on your right. At the end of Nieuwe Doelenstraat, cross the bridge. Below you is the water of the Amstel, the river that lends its name to the city, and ahead is an unmistakeable landmark, the Munttoren.

Built in 1622, the tower is yet another grandiose piece of work by Hendrick de Keyser (1565-1621), whose trademark fancy spires adorn the Westerkerk and the Zuiderkerk. It stands on the site of the Regulierspoort, the original south gate through the town walls. It became the Mint Tower in 1672, when the mint of the Dutch Republic was moved from Utrecht to Amsterdam to save it from the invading armies of Louis XIV of France.

3 At the end of the bridge, with the Munttoren in front of you, turn left and walk along the Amstel quay with the water of the Binnen (Inner) Amstel on your left. The river curves southward, leading you after two long and three very short blocks to the most elegant bridge in Amsterdam. Across the river is the big modern complex that houses the Stadhuis, the Opera and the Muziektheater, familiarly known as the Stopera.

Confusingly, the Blauwe Brug is no longer blue. Built in 1883, it replaced an earlier bridge which was painted in the blue of the Dutch tricolour and the name stuck. Those who have visited Paris may find it looks familiar – it's a copy of Paris's Pont Alexandre, with stone piers shaped like ships' prows and decorative columns topped with mock-Classical capitals and yellow crowns. When it was built, many Amsterdammers condemned the money spent on prettifying it, arguing that a bridge didn't need such fol-de-rols.

4 Cross the bridge on the left side, but pause midway across to look down the river.

DISTANCE 2 miles (3.2km)

ALLOW 3 hours

START Nieuwmarkt

FINISH De Gooier Windmill, corner of Sarphatistraat and Oostenburgergracht

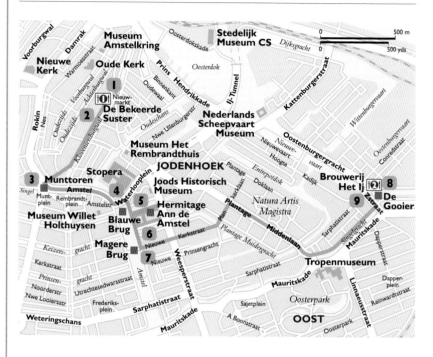

Both banks of the Amstel are lined with houseboats, some of which are 'double-parked'. Houseboats in this area are keenly sought-after dwellings.

5 Turn right, with the river on your right. One short block brings you to the Walter Suskindbrug, which crosses the Nieuwe Herengracht (for more on Suskind see Walk 7). In common with many Amsterdam bridges, the centre sections of this wooden bridge can be raised to allow barges through. Cross

the bridge. To your left, a short distance along the Nieuwe Herengracht's south bank, you will find the former Amstelhof.

Now known as the Hermitage aan de Amstel, this former hospice for elderly people was built in 1681. At the time of writing it was due to reopen in 2009, after an extensive conversion, as a branch of the famous Hermitage Museum in St Petersburg, Russia.

HERMITAGE AAN DE AMSTEL;

www.hermitage.nl

6 Continue along the Amstel. Cross the Nieuwe Keizersgracht to Nieuwe Kerkstraat and another bridge.

The slender Magere Brug is a favourite picture-postcard subject. There has been a bridge here since the 17th century, when the daughters of a wealthy family living on the east side of the Amstel wanted easy access to their stables and coach house on the other bank. The family's name (apparently) was Magere, hence the bridge's name. But *magere* also means 'meagre' or 'skinny', so the name may just as easily come from the original bridge's narrow footway. In 1722 it was widened into a double drawbridge to allow boats to pass on either side. In 1929 it was replaced by a new bridge – which is, however, a faithful copy of the original.

7 Don't cross the bridge. Turn left on Nieuwe Kerkstraat and walk for two long blocks, crossing the busy Weesperstraat midway. At the end of Nieuwe Kerkstraat, cross Plantage Muidergracht and veer left along Plantage Kerklaan for one block. At Plantage Middenlaan, cross over and turn right, with the leafy gardens of the Artis Zoo on your left. Walk all the way to the end of the gardens, recross Plantage Muidergracht and on its opposite bank cross Sarphatistraat and Alexanderplein onto Alexanderkade. With the water of the Singelgracht on your right, walk one long block to reach the corner of Zeeburgerstraat. Ahead is the city's last surviving windmill. At Zeeburgerstraat, turn left and cross the street.

WHERE TO EAT

🍴 **DE BEKEERDE SUSTER,**
Kloveniersburgwal 6-8;
Tel: 020 423 0112.
www.beiaardgroep.nl
This brewery-pub serves its own beers and also has good snacks. €

🍴 **BROUWERIJ HET IJ,**
Funenkade 7;
Tel: 020 622 8325.
www.brouwerijhetij.nl
This brewery-pub next to a famous windmill has its own brews on tap. €

The De Gooier Windmill, also known as the Funenmolen, has been here since 1725. Its thatched wooden frame stands on a brick base. Sadly it is no longer a working mill.

8 Next to the windmill a red brick building displays the ostrich logo of the Brouwerij Het Ij – another of Amsterdam's few surviving independent brewhouse-taverns.

Kaspar Peterson has been brewing beer in this former public baths since 1985 and his selection of five main brews, plus seasonal beers, offers some tasty choices.
BROUWERIJ HET IJ;
Tours FRI, SAT, SUN, at midday
www.brouwerijhetij.nl

9 To return to the city centre, take 10, 22 or 43 trams from the corner of Sarphatistraat and Oostenburgergracht.

THE MAGERE CANTILEVER LIFTING BRIDGE ON THE AMSTEL

De Pijp – Amsterdam's Latin Quarter

De Pijp is home to many immigrant communities and is crammed with places to eat and drink offering Ethiopian, Indonesian and Tibetan cuisine.

The Singelgracht forms a boundary between the historic centre of Amsterdam and its more recently built southern suburbs. The liveliest, most multi-cultural district is that known as De Pijp (the Pipe), occupying a square of densely built-up streets bounded by the Singelgracht to the north, the Amstel river to the east, the Amstelkanaal to the south and the Beoerenwetering to the west. Building south of the Singelgracht began in earnest in the 1870s, when private developers crammed as many narrow streets of cramped four- and five-storey apartment buildings into the available space as they possibly could. Gracious living, it isn't – but De Pijp has an undeniable raffish charm. In the 1890s and the 1900s it was Amsterdam's cabaret district, full of nightclubs, shady bars and houses of ill repute. Oddly enough, most of that trade has migrated to the city centre. Housing here is cheaper than in the centre, and De Pijp is home to many new immigrants to the city. This walk can be combined with Walk 14.

Heineken experience

Take tram 16, 24 or 25 and get off at the first stop after crossing the Singelgracht, on Ferdinand Bolsstraat, which forms the west side of Marie Heinekenplein. For more than a century, this was the home of Heineken lager, one of Amsterdam's better known and most popular exports.

Gerard Adrianus Heineken set up his brewery here in 1868, and by 1930 Heineken had expanded to become De Pijp's biggest employer. The huge brewery buildings occupied several blocks, and the reek of malt hung over the surrounding streets. In 1988, Heineken relocated to more modern premises in Zoeterwoude, out of town. The oldest surviving part of the brewery re-opened in 2008 as the Heineken Experience, but unless you are fascinated by the history of canned lager it is not Amsterdam's most exciting attraction. The square is named after Gerard's cousin, Marie (1844–1930), well known in her lifetime as a painter but not so high profile now.

2 Unless you plan to visit the Heineken Experience, leave Marie Heinekenplein by Eerste Jacob van Campenstraat and walk one short block. Turn left on Frans Halsstraat and walk three blocks, crossing Quellijnstraat and Daniel Stalpertstraat, to Gerard Doustraat. Turn left here.

Paris had Aristide Bruant; Amsterdam had Eduard Jacobs, the 'manure minstrel'. Frans Halsstraat and its side streets were the focus of De Pijp's louche nightlife in the 1890s and 1900s. Jacobs brought cabaret to Amsterdam after visiting Paris's Latin Quarter where he was inspired by the great Bruant. Hugely popular, he was known for his down-and-dirty lyrics of local lowlife, performing at the nightclub De Kuil, which stood at Quellijnstraat 64. He died in 1914.

DISTANCE **1 mile (1.6km)**

ALLOW **1.5 hours**

START **Marie Heinekenplein**

FINISH **Sarphatipark (Ceinturbaan exit)**

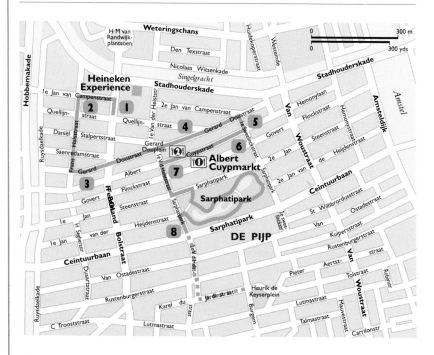

3 Walk along Gerard Doustraat for two blocks, crossing Ferdinand Bolstraat, to Gerard Douplein.

In the centre of the square is a piece of public art that you either love or hate. Three 15ft (4.5m) squiggly monoliths of polished white concrete, studded with brass and glass plaques, are topped by bronze crowns that light up from within at night. Definitely more impressive after dark, this is the work of the Dutch sculptor Henk Duijn, erected in 1995.

4 Continue for two more blocks along the righthand side of Gerard Doustraat. As you pass the corners of Quellijnstraat and Tweede J Van Campenstraat on the opposite side of the street, look across to the street to the peculiar buildings at each corner.

The side streets to the north of Gerard Doustraat were built in the 1870s. They followed the lines of existing paths and drainage ditches, so they joined at sharp angles and the corner houses had to be built on triangular plots – the locals call them 'the cake-slices'.

5 Turn right on Eerste Sweelinckstraat and walk less than 50yd (46m) to the corner of Albert Cuypstraat

On your left at the corner is a bronze statue of a burly bloke, microphone in hand, perched on a bar stool. This is local boy made good Andre Hazes, born in 1951 at 67 Gerard Doustraat. Known as a singer in local cafés from an early age, he finally hit the big time in 1976 with *Eenzame Kerst* (*Lonesome Christmas*) and recorded 36 albums before his death in 2004. Most of his songs are tear-jerkers in the style called *levenslied* ('songs about life'), which have themes similar to the blues or Country and Western – drinking, self-pitying men and the women who love and hate them. A hard drinker himself, he died of heart failure. He still has cult status in the Netherlands.

6 Now turn left into Albert Cuypstraat – the liveliest, loudest and longest street market in Amsterdam. The De Pijp district probably gets its name from this long narrow street, which – before it was drained and filled in – was a drainage ditch for the whole area and known as The Pipe.

The only market in Europe that can really compare with the Albert Cuyp Market is London's Brick Lane. The first barrow-boys started selling their produce here in 1905. It now has more than 260 stalls, open from just after dawn until

6pm every day except Sunday, and on Saturdays it pulls in more than 40,000 buyers and browsers. You can buy just about anything in this multi-ethnic bazaar, from the finest Dutch cheeses to exotic (and sometimes unrecognizable) food and drink from all over the world, and the street is packed with ethnic eating places. Around a century ago, many householders rented rooms to prostitutes and to less respectable tenants such as journalists, authors, artists, students and other riff-raff, who patronized the local

95

WHERE TO EAT

🍴 **ALBERT CUYP 67,**
Albert Cuypstraat 67;
Tel: 020 671 1396.
This basic eatery on the fringe of the
Albert Cuypstraat market doesn't
even have a name, just a street
number, but it does serve cheap and
cheerful Surinamese-Chinese food
– vegetable curries, rice and noodle
dishes, fried banana and plantain. €

🍴 **KISMET,**
Albert Cuypstraat 64;
Tel: 020 671 4768.
Authentic Turkish restaurant with a
great choice of vegetable dishes as
well as grilled meat plates, kebabs and
sticky Turkish desserts. Tables outside
for sunny days. €

cafés and cabarets. This melting pot of
characters and cultures earned De Pijp its
reputation as Amsterdam's Latin Quarter.

7 After browsing your way along
Albert Cuypstraat for one long
block, take the first street on your left,
Eerste van der Helststraat. Follow this
for three very short blocks, crossing
Govert Flinckstraat and Eerste Jan
Steenstraat, and then turn left on
Sarphatipark. After about 50yd (46m),
turn right and enter the park by its
northern entrance.

This patch of greenery, surrounding a
long, thin, man–made pond is named

after Samuel Sarphati (1813-66), the
doctor and philanthropist who played a
big part in re-energizing Amsterdam. He
helped to drag it out of the doldrums that
beset the city in the first half of the 19th
century, after almost a century of military
and naval defeats, foreign occupation, the
loss of colonies such as the Cape Colony,
Mauritius, Ceylon and Malacca to
Britain, and economic decline. Sarphati
was a bundle of do-gooding energy.
He organized a bank, a construction
company, an exhibition centre and a
venture capital company to revitalize the
city's economy, and he cleaned up the
streets by setting up a profitable garbage
removal service, which sold Amsterdam's
leftovers to farmers for pig-swill – today's
eco-warriors would approve.

Facing you as you enter the park is
a monument to Sarphati. Next to it
stands a fanciful little rotunda that looks
more like an ancient Greek monument
than the mundane pump-house that it
actually is. Turn left here to walk round
the pretty little lake with its fountains and
willow trees, and follow the path round
clockwise to bring you back to the west
side of the park.

8 Exit here, and turn left on Eerste
van der Helststraat. At the
south-west corner of the park, cross
Ceinturbaan, a major thoroughfare, to
catch tram 25 or 3 eastbound back to
the city centre. Alternatively, to link this
walk with Walk 15, carry on walking for
three blocks to Karel Du Jardinstraat,
turn left, and walk one block to reach
Henrick De Keijserplein.

OPPOSITE: SARPHATIPARK IN DE PIJP

PAVEMENT CAFÉ IN DE PIJP

A Vision of the Future in De Pijp

Amsterdam architecture is much more than church steeples and 17th-century gables, as this walk through the blocks south of De Pijp will prove.

The unique architectural legacy of Amsterdam's Golden Age, with its canal-side mansions and soaring churches, casts a long shadow. But the city has a more modern legacy of imaginative architecture and town planning, dating from the first half of the 20th century. Population pressure forced the city to expand beyond the Singelgracht – the outermost of its concentric rings of canals – into new territory to the south. This created new opportunities for entrepreneurs and planners. In 1867, the city architect J G van Niftrik drew up a development plan for the district now called De Pijp, between the Singelgracht and the Amstelkanaal (see Walk 13). The northern part was set for high-density housing, while the southern sector was for more expensive homes. Instead, by the 1920s, social-democratic ideals had taken hold and many of the most striking complexes were built by the new housing associations. The result is superb architecture of the adventurous Amsterdam School, which flourished between 1910-25.

1 Take tram 25 to the stop at the corner of Ceintuurbaan and Eerste van der Helststraat (at the south-west corner of Sarphatipark). Cross Ceintuurbaan and walk down Tweede van der Helststraat to Van der Helstplein. This small square is filled with massive trees whose foliage completely covers it in summer.

Tweede van der Helstraat, with its buildings of different heights and styles, constructed with no overall plan is typical of the Oude Pijp, but as you cross this small square, you leave behind the higgledy-piggledy architecture of the Oude Pijp. The buildings to your left as you enter the square are typical of planned, harmonious architecture of the Nieuwe Pijp. In the middle of the square is another piece of public art: an ellipse of blue concrete blocks dotted with concealed spotlights. Anneliese Dijkman, the artist, aimed to soften the square's harsh lines with this work, called *In 't Blauw* (*In the Blue*).

2 Turn left along Karel Du Jardinstraat and walk one block to Hendrick de Keijserplein.

This rather undistinguished square is named in homage to the first and greatest of Dutch architects of the Golden Age. Hendrick de Keyser (1565-1621) architect, master builder and father of the Amsterdam Renaissance style, designed three of Amsterdam's greatest churches – the Westerkerk, Zuiderkerk and the Noorderkerk – as well as two other prominent landmarks, the Munttoren and the Montelbanstoren.

3 Turn right, walk down the west side of the square, cross Lutmastraat and walk down Burgemeester Tellegenstraat. Take the next left turning into the Cooperatiehof.

The Cooperatiehof was designed by Piet Kramer (1881-1961), one of the leading architects of the Amsterdam School, as an educational centre and meeting place for workers living in the new housing complex nearby – built by the co-operative social housing corporation De Dageraad (The Dawn). In many ways, it's a monument to pragmatic working-class self-improvement. In the 1920s, the politically aware workers of Amsterdam knew that if they wanted decent homes they would have to build them themselves, and formed associations like De Dageraad to do so. On your right is the Cooperatiehof's library and reading room, with a rooftop clock tower that was intended to symbolize working-class educational ambitions.

4 Leave the Cooperatiehof by its eastern exit, and turn diagonally right. You are now back on Burgemeester Tellegenstraat. Follow this to the corner of P L Takstraat, the next street on your left.

A monument to Jan Willem Cornelis Tellegen stands at this crossroads. As Social-Democrat Mayor of Amsterdam from 1915-21, he pushed through a

OPPOSITE: GARDENS OF DE DAGERAAD APARTMENT COMPLEX

14

DISTANCE 1.5 miles (2.4km)

ALLOW 2 hours

START Ceintuurbaan/Sarphatipark

FINISH Ceintuurbaan/Amsteldijk

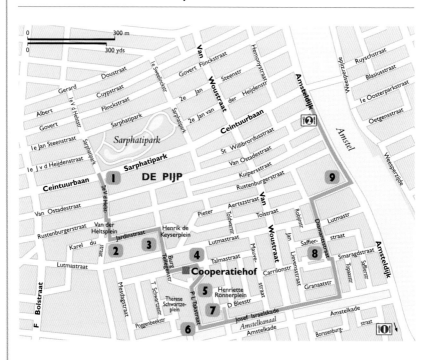

revolution in social housing that left its stamp on this part of the city.

5 Turn left on P L Takstraat. This street is an outstanding treasury of architecture and design that was revolutionary in its day. It's a 1920s social-modernist's vision of the future, a million miles away from the picture-postcard architecture of the city centre.

Unlike most town-planners in Britain and elsewhere, Piet Kramer and other

architects of the Amsterdam School thought purpose-built workers' housing should be decorative as well as purely functional. The result is a unique style that seems to combine the curves and quirks of Art Deco with elements of socialist inspirational art. Two huge, round apartment blocks built in the 1920s dominate the street. On your left as you look down the street from the monument is a sculpted eagle, symbolizing the ascent of the working class; on the right is an idealized sculpture of a labourer.

With its undulating lines and quirky embellishments – abstract patterns in stone and vertically laid brick, round balconies, lead cockerels topping roof cornices, eccentrically shaped windows and doorways – the architecture is also reminiscent of Kramer's contemporary, Gaudi, in Barcelona.

The street reaches an architectural climax in the buildings of the H P Berlage School, which straddle P L Takstraat. Each building is crowned by a remarkable complex of sculptures. On the right, *De geboorte van de daad* (*The Birth of the Deed*) is a riot of forms that clearly show the influence of ancient Egyptian art: horses, human figures, a woman's face and a newborn baby. On the left, *Menselijke energie* (*Human Energy*) symbolizes commerce, agriculture, industry and the future. Both are the work of Hildo Krop, Amsterdam's town sculptor from 1916 to 1970.

6 At the end of P L Takstraat turn left along Jozef Israelskade, keeping to the opposite side from the Amstelkanaal. After one short block, take the first left into Henriette Ronnerplein. With the buildings along Takstraat, this is the heart of the Dageraad complex, built in 1923.

Piet Kramer worked with another pioneer of the Amsterdam School, Michel de Klerk, to create this striking housing complex. The single-family dwellings on the left side of Henriette Ronnerplein represented a breakthrough in a city where workers traditionally lived in rented apartments. But these small houses are linked by walls and connecting balconies, combining community with individualism. Beneath each balcony, bricks form the words *De Dageraad*.

The architects had a priggish sense of what was best for working-class families. They wanted to keep people at home,

off the street and out of the taverns, so they placed windows high up to prevent people from leaning out to chat with neighbours or passers-by. There were no bathrooms and kitchens were tiny, to discourage people from washing themselves in the sink.

7 Return to Josef Israelskade, turn left, and walk three blocks, with the Amstelkanaal on your right, to Diamantstraat. Turn left here and walk two short blocks to the corner of Diamantstraat and Smaragdstraat.

The flying saucer-shaped building on your right was, in fact, a public bath-house, built in 1926, when most working-class homes lacked bathrooms. By the 1950s the average Amsterdammer took a bath around 10 times a year, but by then more homes had hot water and bathrooms of their own, and use of the public baths declined.

8 Continue along Diamantstraat, the main drag of the Diamantbuurt, the former Diamond Quarter, for three short blocks, past the cottages built for workers at the Diamantslijperij Asscher, and turn right onto Tolstraat. Facing each other halfway along the block are two striking buildings.

With its kitsch battlements and multiple windows, the Asscher diamond factory, built in 1910, looks like a fake-medieval castle. The innovative eight-sided 'Asscher cut' made the company wealthy in the early 20th century and it was here that

WHERE TO EAT

[O] CTASTE AMSTERDAM,
Amsteldijk 55;
Tel: 06223 35366.
www.ctaste.nl
In this unique restaurant you eat in total darkness. The experience is said to heighten your sense of taste, smell, sound and texture. €€

[O] LE HOLLANDAIS,
Amsteldijk 41;
Tel: 020 679 1248.
www.lehollandais.nl
Michelin-starred restaurant serving French cuisine with dishes such as navarin of lamb and fried brill with sea urchins and morels. Open for dinner only, from 6pm. €€€

the largest diamond ever found, the Cullinan, was cut in 1908 before being mounted in the British crown jewels.

Opposite the former Asscher works, on the south side of the street, is another gem of 1920s futurism. Now a public library, the CineTol was built in 1927 for the Theosophical Association, one of the leading pseudo-religions of the time. It later become a cinema, and is a classic example of the New Realist style.

9 At the end of Tolstraat, turn left and walk along Amsteldijk, with the river on your right, for four very short blocks to Ceintuurbaan. From the corner of Ceintuurbaan and Amsteldijk tram 3 takes you back to the city centre.

Exploring the Western Islands

Amsterdam's manmade islands have gone from working docklands to the coolest place to live in the city. There's even an artificial beach.

The Westelijk Eilanden (Western Islands) are only a short walk from Centraal Station and the bustling city centre, but until very recently this district west of the Westerdok was – like docklands the world over – a self-contained working-class community with an identity of its own. Since the 1990s, that identity has been diluted and gentrification has proceeded apace, with old warehouses being converted into apartments for upwardly mobile couples, and houses with views over the river commanding premium prices. The hub of the district is Prinseneiland (Princes' Island), created in the 17th century by the dredging of the Westerdok. Merchants whose trading vessels docked here built their homes along the quayside so that they could keep an eye on business. Typically, they kept an office on the ground floor, lived on the second and third floors, and stored their goods in the loft above. Many older houses have stout wooden beams jutting from their gables, used to hoist sacks straight off the ship and into the attic. This walk is at its best in summer – bring your swimming gear.

1 Take the metro or bus to Centraal Station. This walk starts outside Centraal Station's rear entrance. Leave the station and turn left along De Ruijterkade with the River Ij on your right.

The buildings of Centraal Station block off the city centre from the broad open reach of the Ij (pronounced 'Eye') estuary so effectively that it comes as some surprise to confront Amsterdam's corridor to the North Sea, bustling with barges and cross-river ferries. The quay is named after Michiel de Ruyter (1607–76), one of the greatest Dutch admirals of the 17th century and a man who, it seems, would fight anybody. Son of a beer porter from Vlissingen, he ran away to sea at the age of 11, became a trader, merchant skipper, occasional privateer and eventually a great commander of Dutch fleets, leading his ships against the Spanish, the French, the English, the Swedes and the Barbary corsairs in the Mediterranean, the North Sea, the Baltic and the Caribbean. His men loved him: they nicknamed him *Bestevaer* (Grandpa). He was still in action at the age of 69, when he was killed at the battle of Agosta. He is buried in the Nieuwe Kerk, alongside other Dutch heroes. His body was hastily and not very effectively embalmed – when one of his descendants opened his casket in 1948 he was distressed to discover that De Ruyter's leg, severed by the French cannonball that killed him, had not been re-attached or correctly positioned, but just tossed into the coffin with the rest of the body.

2 Follow De Ruijterkade past the station building, over the bridge that crosses the mouth of the Open Haven, and turn left onto the broad underpass beneath the railway tracks, onto Droogbak. At the end of Droogbak, turn right on Haarlemmer Houttuinen. Follow this regrettably dull and busy main road for one long block, with the railway on your right, until you reach the first turning on your right. Turn right here, under the railway bridge (which usually displays some fine examples of colourful cutting-edge spray-can graffiti) to Hendrik Jonkerplein. Walk diagonally across the small square and turn right along Bickersgracht, keeping the canal on your left.

The canals that separate the artificial islands and peninsulas of the Westelijk Eilanden are berths for the biggest fleet of houseboats in Amsterdam. They range from small 'do-it-yourself' floating homes built on rusting pontoons rafts to converted *tjalks* (seagoing barges), tugboats, and more ostentatious purpose-built cruisers.

On your right, on the second block of this street of unassuming canal-side apartment blocks, keep your ears open for unexpected farmyard sounds. Stadsboerderij De Dierencapel, at No. 27, is a city farm, with an assortment of chickens, ducks, pigs, goats, sheep and rabbits. Admission is free and time spent here getting to know the animals is guaranteed to please children.

CITY FARM;
TUE-SUN 9-4.30. Tel: 020 645 5034

15

DISTANCE **2.5 miles (4km)**

ALLOW **3.5 hours**

START **Centraal Station**

FINISH **Centraal Station**

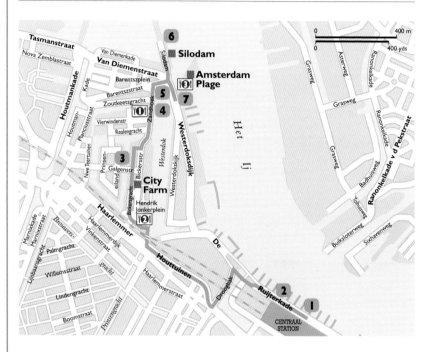

3 Leaving the farm, turn right again on Bickersgracht. At its northern end, veer right, then left to cross beneath the goalpost-like white steel gantries of the Zandhoekbrug, then carry on along Zandhoek.

Side by side along this quayside are the most enviable homes on the Western Islands, a row of gracious 17th-century houses with elegant white stucco doorways and window surrounds. At the other end of the spectrum, but almost equally as enviable, are the sturdy old sailing barges that have been converted into charming houseboats and are moored along the dockside.

At the corner of Zandhoek and Vierwindenstraat, on your left, is De Goudene Real. Now a stylish restaurant, it was once the home of 16th-century merchant, Jacob Real, and on its gable-stone is a carved and painted gold coin – a Spanish *real*, in fact, and another of those visual name puns of which Amsterdammers were so fond.

4 At the north end of Zandhoek, cross another white-painted drawbridge, the Far Zandhoekbrug, across Zoutkeetsgracht, to find yourself almost immediately on the small triangle of Barentzsplein.

Several of the streets on the Western Islands are named after great Dutch explorers. Willem Barentsz (1550-97) led three voyages into the Arctic Ocean in search of a north-east passage to Asia. He failed, and on his third voyage died after his ship became trapped in the ice, but the Barents Sea is named after him. To your left off the square,

Van Diemenstraat is named after Antony Van Diemen, Governor of the Dutch East India Company's possessions in the 1630s, whose protégé Abel Tasman circumnavigated Australia for the first time in 1642-43. Tasman also found a large island which he named after his patron. In the 18th century, under British rule, Van Diemen's Land became a notoriously brutal prison colony, and in 1835 British settlers renamed it Tasmania, hoping to expunge its evil reputation. Tasman also became the first European to discover New Zealand, naming it after a Dutch province, and he too has a street named after him here.

ABOVE: BICKERSEILAND ZANDHOEK HOUSEBOATS

5 Turn right on Barentszstraat (the south side of Barentzsplein), cross Van Diemenstraat, and turn left on Silodam. On your right, and unmistakable, is one of Amsterdam's newest and most adventurous slices of architecture.

Built in 2002, the Silodam looks more like a huge container ship than the residential complex it is. Ten storeys high, it contains 157 flats – each with its own balcony and tiny patio garden. Bold primary colours alternate with steel, glass and aluminium. It's the kind of innovative design you either love or hate. Judging by the rents and the length of the waiting list for apartments here, plenty of people love it. The older part of the complex was originally a huge grain warehouse, known simply as The Silo, and from the 1970s to the late 1980s was one of the city's most famous and successful squatter communities, with performance spaces, art studios, a restaurant, shops and one of the city's best music and dance venues as well as residential homes.

6 On a hot summer's day, a welcome surprise awaits at the end of this walk. Cross Silodam to the riverside, turn right, and on your left is, of all things, a beach.

Amsterdam Plage is, admittedly, artificial and made of sand dredged from the river bed – but then, so is most of Amsterdam. Every summer, tons of sand are dumped by the authorities on the Stenen Hoofd, a wide and otherwise disused pier that juts out into the River Ij, turning it into a temporary seaside in the city, complete with outdoor entertainment and places to eat and drink. Slap on some suntan lotion and hang out with the locals.

AMSTERDAM PLAGE;
MID-JUN - MID-SEP 11-11 DAILY
www.amsterdamplage.nl

7 A 10-minute walk south on Westerdoksdijk, then De Ruijterkade, will bring you back to Centraal Station.

WHERE TO EAT

|○| DE GOUDEN REAL,
Zandhoek 14;
Tel: 020 623 3883.
Posh restaurant overlooking the Westerdok and IJ. Classic French dishes in gracious surroundings. €€€

|○| CAFÉ 'T BLAAUHOOFT,
Hendrick Jonckerplein 1;
Tel: 020 632 8721.
www.blaauwhooft.nl
Attractive, friendly café-restaurant on Bickerseiland. Excellent seafood and Indonesian-influenced dishes. €€

|○| AMSTERDAM PLAGE CANTINA,
Stenen Hoofd, Westerdoksdijk;
Tel: 06 4429 1662.
www.amsterdamplage.nl
Cold drinks, snacks and light meals served on Amsterdam's summer-only city beach. €

OPPOSITE: SILODAM RESIDENTIAL COMPLEX

MUZIE

Jordaan – the Artists' Quarter

This walk takes in a rainbow assortment of Amsterdam's galleries, from rock iconography to graffiti, sculpture to Chagall lithographs.

Ever since Rembrandt (1606-69), Amsterdam has been a city of artists and art dealers. It's easy to forget that in his day Rembrandt was an art revolutionary, daring to do things with paint, pencil and stylus that no artist before him had achieved. That tradition continues. Amsterdam is one of the world's great creative capitals, humming with talent and dotted with galleries that show the latest in experimental art, from painting and print-making to sculpture, photography and an ever-expanding portfolio of new media. The bohemian Jordaan has been a hotbed of artistic talent for more than half a century, and its narrow streets are crammed with artists' studios and galleries that foster cutting-edge work by artists from all over the world. Art aficionados will be in heaven here, and even if you're not a serious collector there is a huge assortment of work by contemporary artists. There are at least 100 galleries and studios in the Jordaan – it's impossible to do justice to them all, so this is just a selection. The galleries are not far apart, making this a good walk for a cold or rainy day.

I Take tram 13 or 17 to the corner of Rozengracht and Lijnbaansgracht. Don't cross the street or the canal bridge. Turn left and walk along Lijnbaansgracht for three very short blocks to Lauriergracht, the first small canal on your left. Don't cross it. Turn left and walk along Lauriergracht with the canal on your right. About halfway along the second block, at No. 94, is the Torch Gallery.

Torch is one of Amsterdam's most exciting new art spaces, specializing in works by photographers and new media artists. Adriaan van der Have's gallery is not always for the easily shocked: exhibitors have included Anton Corbijn, one of the top lensmen of the great rock years of the 1970s and 1980s, but also US porno actress turned snapper Annie Sprinkle and Nazi film-maker Leni Riefenstahl (1902-2003).

TORCH GALLERY;
THU-SAT 2-6 and by appointment
www.torchgallery.com

2 Carry on in the same direction to the end of Lauriergracht, where it meets Prinsengracht. Turn left, pass Laurierstraat on your left, then take the next left into Rozenstraat. About three quarters of the way up the next block, at No. 59, is the Stedelijk Museum Bureau Amsterdam.

Founded in 1993, SMBA is an offshoot of the Stedelijk Museum (see Walk 8). Its aim is to present contemporary art from Amsterdam's point of view as well as in a global context. Curator Jelle Bouwhuis presents an ever-changing kaleidoscope of shows and residency programmes – never boring, always challenging, occasionally infuriating.

STEDELIJK MUSEUM BUREAU AMSTERDAM;
TUE-SUN 11-5 www.smba.nl

3 Walk along Rozenstraat to the corner of Eerste Rozendwaarstraat. Turn right. Halfway down the very short and narrow street, on your right at No. 10, is the exhibition centre for one of the Jordaan's most exciting art initiatives.

Some of the most exciting work by a number of Amsterdam's most adventurous art-makers goes on show for three days every other year on Pentecost weekend. Open Studios Jordaan is a moveable feast, when around 70 artists and art collectives open their studios to visitors, with a central exhibition displaying samples of their work. You can find details of all the participating artists on the Open Studios website and even if your next visit doesn't coincide with their next event, the site still showcases work by many of the city's most exciting talents.

www.openateliersjordaan.nl

4 At Rozengrachtsdwaartstraat, turn right and cross Rozengracht, walk one very short block up Tweede Bloemendwaarstraat, and turn left onto Bloemstraat. On your left at No. 140 is Galerie Fons Welters, behind a modernistic chocolate brown and aluminium façade.

16

DISTANCE **1.5 miles (2.4km)**

ALLOW **2 hours**

START **Rozengracht/Lijnbaansgracht**

FINISH **Westermarkt**

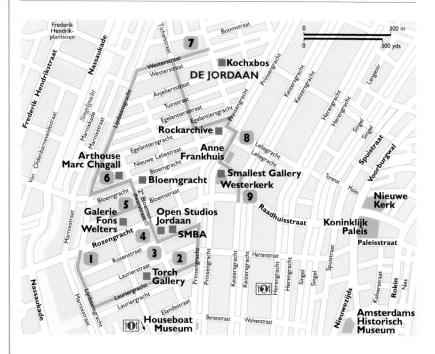

Fons Welters opened his gallery in 1988 and since then has fostered the work of some of the most promising young talent working in Amsterdam, exhibiting paintings by artists such as Rob Birza, Claire Harvey, Eylem Aladogan, Daniel Roth and many others.

Work on show may range from Birza's colourful, almost comic-book canvases to Tom Claassen's witty, animal and humanoid sculpture, Clair Harvey's tiny works on Post-it notes or Aladogan's eldritch three-dimensional works in leather, felt, wood, metal and ceramic.

GALERIE FONS WELTERS;
TUE-SAT 1-7 www.fonswelters.nl

5 Retrace your steps to Tweede Bloemendwaarstraat, walk one very short block to Bloemgracht. Cross the canal. Arthouse Marc Chagall is across the road on the corner opposite the bridge, just to your left.

Leo Verdegaal opened this gallery in 1999 after many years of collecting graphic works by Marc Chagall. He specializes in lithographs and other graphic art by Chagall, and many are surprisingly affordable because they are unsigned works from longer runs, but sold with unconditional guarantees of authenticity. Born Moishe Shagal in 1887 in Liozna (then part of Russia, now in Belarus), Chagall renamed himself while studying in Paris before World War I. He returned to Russia after the Bolshevik Revolution of 1917, when he became Commissar for Fine Art in his native Belarus, a post that he resigned two years later after clashing with his contemporary Kazimir Malevich. Chagall's often whimsical symbolism was utterly at odds with Malevich's relentlessly abstract Suprematist ideas of art (some of which you can see in Walk 8). From Moscow, Chagall returned to Paris, escaping to New York in 1941 ahead of the German invasion and returning to France in 1948. He spent most of the rest of his life in Provence, where he died in 1985. 'I work in whatever medium likes me at the moment', Chagall said, and his work spans a number of different media including graphic art, like the prints sold here, stained glass, painted works, murals and mosaics.

ARTHOUSE MARC CHAGALL;
THU-SAT 12-6 www.chagallkunst.com

6 Leave the gallery, keep the water on your left, and follow Bloemgracht, past the post office on your right, back to Lijnbaansgracht. Turn right, and walk six very short blocks north to reach Westerstraat, crossing the water of the

WHERE TO EAT

🍽 FESTINA LENTE,
Looiersgracht 40B.
Tel: 020 638 1412.
Friendly, laid-back café-bar serving snacks and drinks, with tables outside in summer. €

🍽 DE ADMIRAAL,
Herengracht 319;
Tel: 020 625 4334.
Perk up your day with a shot of *geniever* from Van Wees, the last independent distiller in Amsterdam, in this super *proeflokaal* café bar. Outdoor terrace for sunny days. €

Bloemgracht and Egelantiersgracht on the way. At Westerstraat, turn right, and walk one block to Tichelstraat. Cross Tichelstraat, continue to the end of the next block, and Kochxbos is on your right just after the corner, at Eerste Anjeliersdwarstraat 3-5.

Be afraid… be very afraid. Unless, of course, you love highly original graphic design, lowbrow and underground art. Esther Koch and Hans Bos merge the streetwise aesthetics of graffiti, fantasy art and inventive 21st-century surrealism.

KOCHXBOS;
WED-SAT 1-6 www.kochxbos.nl

7 Retrace your steps to Tichelstraat and turn left, crossing Anjeliersstraat, Tuinstraat, Egelantiersstraat and the water of

Egelantiersgracht. On the south side of Egelantiersgracht, turn left and walk one block to the corner of Egelantiersgracht and Prinsengracht. Cross back over Egelantiersgracht by the small canal bridge and on the corner, at Prinsengracht 110, is Rockarchive.

Snapper Jill Furmanovsky is a rock 'n' roll legend in her own right and has been hanging out with the greatest for more than 30 years. In 1998, she launched Rockarchive, a chain of galleries (there are also branches in London and Dublin) dedicated to the bold, bad and beautiful of rock and roll, from Afrika Bambaataa to Led Zeppelin and everyone in between. Limited edition images of rock's greatest icons at affordable prices.

ROCKARCHIVE;

WED-FRI 2-6, SAT 12-6 www.rockarchive.com

8 Cross Prinsengracht and walk with the canal on your right, past the Anne Frank House, and turn left onto the north side of Westermarkt, opposite the exit from the Anne Frank House.

The Smallest Gallery, at Westermarkt 60, is the workspace of artist Sonja Bolten, whose cheerful, vivid pictures of Amsterdam life jostle for space on its walls. Sonja has been painting in Amsterdam for more than 20 years. Her work celebrates its playful, innocent side.

THE SMALLEST GALLERY;

FRI-MON 11-5 www.smallestgallery.com

9 Leaving Westermarkt, cross Raadhuisstraat to take tram 13, 14 or 17 back to the city centre or walk four blocks east on Raadhuisstraat to return to the Dam.

OPPOSITE: THE SMALLEST GALLERY; ABOVE: DISPLAY WITHIN THE ROCKARCHIVE

Weird and Wonderful Museums

Keyboards, bibles, houseboats, cats and handbags – there's a museum celebrating each and every one in Amsterdam.

Amsterdam's museums and art galleries are world famous. Most visitors, of course, put a visit to the Rijksmuseum, the Van Gogh Museum, the Maritime Museum or the Stedelijk Museum at the top of their list. But, as you will discover on this walk, Amsterdam also has a portfolio packed with museums that are eclectic, eccentric and illuminating. They have one thing in common – whether their subject matter is the world of the Old Testament, mankind's love of cats or womankind's love of handbags – all of them have been created by people with a passionate love of the things they collect, and an eager desire to share their passion with the rest of the world. This walk zig-zags from the funky Jordaan, along the inner canal rings that characterize Amsterdam, and back into the heart of the city. On the way, it opens windows into some of the world's odder aspects – from the Holy Land in ancient times to funkadelia to the semiotics of fashion accessories.

1 Take tram 3 or 10 and alight at the Marnixbad tram stop, near the corner of Westerstraat and Lijnbaansgracht. Turn your back to the Singelgracht, cross the Lijnbaansgracht by the Westerstraat bridge. Proceed eastwards along the north side of Westerstraat for two blocks. Cross Tweede Lindendwaarstraat. The first of our weird and wonderful museums, the Pianola Museum, is on your left, just past the corner, at Westerstraat 106.

There is something slightly spooky about a piano that plays itself. Curator Kasper Janse will introduce you to the museum's collection of these strange and beautiful instruments, forerunners of the juke-box. More than two million were made, many of them by the Tonk brothers in New York – hence 'honky tonk', as in *It wasn't God who made Honky Tonk Angels* (recorded by Kitty Wells in 1952) or the even more famous *Honky Tonk Women* by the Rolling Stones in 1969. When the pianola was invented, it looked like the future of music, and major composers including Stravinsky and Hindemith even wrote pieces specially for the pianola.

PIANOLA MUSEUM;
SUN 2-5 and by appointment. www.pianola.nl

2 Turn left as you leave the Pianola Museum and follow Tweede Lindendwaarstraat across Westerstraat, Anjeliersstraat and Tuinstraat to Egelantiersstraat, then turn left to the corner of Prinsengracht. Turn right and cross the water of Egelantiersgracht. The next museum is at the corner of Prinsengracht and Egelantiersgracht, at Prinsengracht 112.

Dedicated to four centuries of the flower that everyone identifies with Amsterdam, from the Tulip Fever of the 17th century – when speculators poured millions into ever newer and more flamboyant varieties – to the present day, and the ongoing search for a black tulip (see also Walk 9).

TULIP MUSEUM;
TUE-SUN 10-6
www.amsterdamtulipmuseum.com

3 Turn left out of the Tulip Museum and walk west on the south side of Egelantiersgracht. Cross Eerste Leliebloemstraat, and turn left onto Tweede Leliebloemsdwaarstraat. On the corner, at No. 5, is Electric Ladyland.

As soon as you enter this one-off art gallery and museum of fluorescent art, you become a glowing part of the art. The museum's name is a tip of the hat to one of rock's greatest guitarists, Jimi Hendrix, who will always be remembered as the king of psychedelia. Upstairs is a gallery of poster art going back to the great days of the acid 1960s, while downstairs dull lumps of rock explode into vivid colours at the flip of a switch.

ELECTRIC LADYLAND;
TUE-SAT 1-6 www.electric-ladyland.com

4 On leaving Electric Ladyland, turn left and walk down Tweede Leliebloemsdwaarstraat, crossing Nieuwe Leliestraat, Bloemgracht and Bloemstraat, to Rozengracht. Turn left

DISTANCE 1.5 miles (2.4km)

ALLOW 4 hours including museum visits

START Marnixbad

FINISH Rembrandtplein

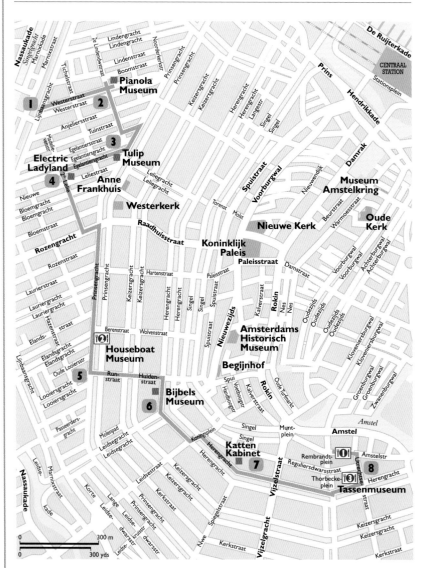

here, then turn right on Prinsengracht, keeping the canal on your left, and walk five blocks along the canal, past (on your right) Rozenstraat, Laurierstraat, Lauriergracht and Elandsstraat. The Houseboat Museum is moored opposite Prinsengracht 296, facing Elandsgracht.

There are around 2,400 floating homes moored along the city's canalsides. But houseboat living is quite a recent phenomenon. In the 1960s, Amsterdam experienced a severe housing shortage. At the same time, thousands of the barges that had carried coal, sand, gravel, beer and other cargoes across the Netherlands were being decommissioned as road and rail supplanted canal transport. So apartments were expensive and in short supply, while boats were cheap and plentiful. Barge skippers and their families traditionally lived aboard, so the vessels were already equipped with galley kitchens and sleeping accommodation – in fact, they were more spacious than many city apartments.

HOUSEBOAT MUSEUM;

MAR-OCT, TUE-SUN 11-5; NOV-FEB, FRI-SUN 11-5 www.houseboatmuseum.nl

5 Carry on along Prinsengracht to the next bridge, at Runstraat. Turn left, across the canal. Walk one very short block to Keizersgracht. Cross this canal, walk one block along Huidenstraat to the corner of Herengracht, and turn right. Midway down the block, at Herengracht 366-368, the Bijbels Museum is housed in two gracious 17th-century buildings.

These houses, built for wealthy merchant Jacob Cromhout in 1662, now house one of the oldest museums in the Netherlands. Its founder, the Rev Leendert Schouden, wanted to bring the bible to life. Today, he would no doubt have had a website, but in the 19th century he commissioned meticulous scale models of Old Testament temples. His attention to detail was obsessive – the sand around his scale model of the

WHERE TO EAT

|O| CAFÉ SCHILLER/BRASSERIE SCHILLER,
Rembrandtplein 36;
Tel: 020 624 9864.
Traditional Dutch and French dishes.
Next-door cafe serves snacks. €€

|2| HOUSEBOAT MUSEUM CAFÉ,
Prinsengracht 296;
Tel: 020 427 0750.
Tea, coffee and soft drinks aboard a
typical converted canal barge. €

|O| TASSENMUSEUM,
Herengracht 573;
Tel: 020 524 645.
www.tassenmuseum.nl
Stylish café overlooking the garden
behind the Handbag Museum. €€

ancient tabernacle was brought all the
way from the Sinai Desert.
BIJBELS MUSEUM;
MON-SAT 10-5, SUN 11-5
www.bijbelsmuseum.nl

6 Exiting the Bijbels Museum, turn
right and walk along Herengracht,
with the water on your left. Cross
Leidsegracht, walk on for a further
block, and at Koningsplein turn left and
cross to the other side of Herengracht.
Turn right, and midway along the next
block turn left into Herengracht 497.

Cat lover William Meijer founded this
charming little museum in 1990. It's
packed with paintings, drawings, prints
and sculptures of cats, and a resident
tribe of five fabulous felines share the
premises. Built in 1667, the house has a
history in its own right – John Adams,
later US President, stayed here in 1780,
when he was the first US envoy to
the Netherlands. Adams persuaded the
Netherlands to recognize the US as an
independent state and wangled a five
million guilder loan to finance the War
of Independence against Britain.
CAT MUSEUM;
TUE-FRI 10-2, SAT-SUN 1-5 www.kattenkabinet.nl

7 Carry on along the north side of
Herengracht, with the canal on your
right, for two and a half blocks, crossing
Vijzelstraat and Thorbeckeplein, to
Herengracht 573 – on your left just
before the corner of Utrechtsestraat.

Entering this quirky museum, you may
feel that you have wandered on to the
set of *Sex and the City*. Hendrikje Ivo
must be the only woman to have been
honoured by her nation for collecting
handbags – she was created a dame of the
Netherlands in 2007. The Tassenmuseum
(Museum of Bags and Purses) has a
collection of 3,000, spanning 200 years.
MUSEUM OF BAGS AND PURSES;
DAILY 10-5 www.tassenmuseum.nl

8 Turn north on Utrechtsestraat,
cross the Herengracht once again,
pass Reguliersdwaarsstraat on your left.
Take the next left into Rembrandtplein
for a huge choice of places to eat and
drink, as well as trams in all directions.

Amsterdamse Bos – A Walk in the Park

It's only a couple of miles from the city centre, but the Amsterdamse Bos is a delightful secret that few visitors are lucky enough to discover.

This great swathe of greenery, more than a mile (1.6km) across at its widest and almost 4 miles (6.4km) long, interspersed with lakes, pools, streams and almost 90 miles (145km) of footpaths, is only a 10-minute bus ride from the inner city, just west of the modern suburb of Amstelveen. It's undeniably at its best in summer (bring a picnic to make the most of it), but it is also a great place for a brisk walk and a breath of fresh air on a winter's day. The Amsterdamse Bos is a product of the Depression years of the 1920s, when it was conceived as a project that would create 'five years work for a thousand men' and give the city its greatest ever green space, on land reclaimed from the sea. Landscape architects C van Esteren and J H Mulder were influenced by the style of great English parks and gardens such as Richmond Common or Windsor Great Park and they aimed to create a planned wilderness that would provide a refuge for birds and wildlife – as well as recreation for humans. Nature lovers will find that it's well worth bringing a pair of binoculars on this walk.

Take bus 170 or 172 from Centraal Station to Van Nijenrodeweg bus stop. The entrance to the park is at the corner of Bosbaan and Van Nijenrodeweg, about 350yd (320m) west of the bus stop. Enter the park to find yourself between two large modern buildings. On the right is the Grand Café de Bosbaan; turn left to enter the Bezoekerscentrum het Bosmuseum (Bosmuseum Visitor Centre).

The visitor centre offers maps and information about activities and events in the Amsterdamse Bos – these include ice skating in winter, nude sunbathing, swimming and canoeing in summer and cycling with rented bikes all year round. It also fills you in on the history. The park was first planned in the 1920s, when newly created *polder* (land reclaimed from the sea) became available and the idea of creating much needed recreational space for Amsterdammers was suggested. The Amsterdamse Bos is some 12ft (3.6m) below sea level. Work began in 1929 and the park opened in 1934, so the oldest trees in what is now a real manmade forest are more than 70 years old. However, planting went on for several decades and the final tree was planted as recently as 1967. The Amsterdamse Bos now has 150 different native trees and plants as well as an exotic arboretum, and it shelters more than 200 bird species.

AMSTERDAMSE BOS;

DAILY 12-5 www.amsterdamsebos.nl

2 Turn left out of the visitor centre, then follow the Bosbaanweg as it

WHERE TO EAT

🍴 GRAND CAFÉ DE BOSBAAN, Bosbaan 4;
Tel: 020 404 4869.
This big lakeside terrace café just next to the park entrance serves pancakes, meals, drinks and snacks. €

🍴 BOERDERIJ MEERZICHT, Koenenkade 56;
Tel: 020 679 2744.
www.boerderijmeerzicht.nl
Located in a pretty farmhouse-style building, Boerderij Meerzicht specializes in sweet and savoury pancake meals. €

curves round towards the waterside and follow the path along the south side of the Bosbaan.

This body of water looks too regular to be natural, and it is of course manmade – a 50yd (46m) wide, 1,000yd (914m) long canal to nowhere that formed part of the original land reclamation project. It is now popular with carp fishermen, swimmers and canoeists in summer, and with skaters in winter.

On the south side of the Bosbaan, on your left, is mature woodland – look out for plentiful bird life in summer, including jays and woodpeckers; on the canal you can expect to spot great crested grebes, coots, mallard and moorhens. From its north side, the Bosbaan drains into a larger artificial lake, the Nieuwe Meer, which forms the northern

129

DISTANCE **5 miles (8km)**

ALLOW **Half a day**

START **Van Nijenrodeweg**

FINISH **Van Nijenrodeweg**

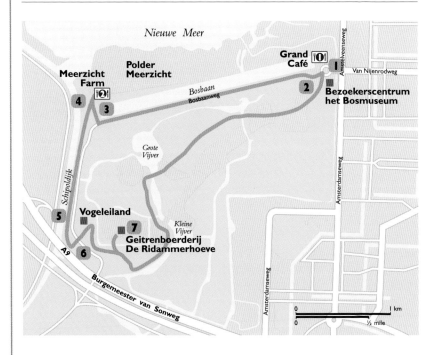

boundary of the Amsterdamse Bos. Midway along the Bosbaanweg, looking north across the water, you can see a wide expanse of low-lying reedbeds. This is the Polder Meerzicht, a typical example of the manmade water-meadows created by the draining of land below sea level. The reedbeds are an important nesting and over-wintering site for many bird species, and in summer they are scattered with orchids and other wild flowers. Much of the Netherlands is polder land, reclaimed from the sea by first enclosing shallow

areas of water with artificial dykes, then pumping out the water from the enclosed space. Maintaining dykes is a constant process, and the threat of rising sea levels caused by climate change is a very real future challenge for the Netherlands.

3 For a closer view of the polder and an encounter with animals, walk on a further 500yd (457m) to the west end of the Bosbaan. Turn right at the end of the canal, with the car park on your left, and walk around 100yd (91m) north.

Ahead is a farmhouse with a red tiled roof, Dutch gables and dormer windows, surrounded by gardens and paddocks.

The Meerzicht Farm is more a visitor attraction than a working farm. Decorative inmates include a flock of peacocks and a family of fallow deer, as well as chickens and rabbits. It also has an excellent pancake restaurant.

4 Walk back to the car park at the west end of the Bosbaan and turn right, to follow the footpath which runs along the Schipholdijk, the narrow channel that forms the west boundary of the Amsterdamse Bos and which flows into the Nieuwe Meer at its north end. Looking ahead (and up) you can't miss the steady stream of aircraft taking off and landing from Amsterdam Schiphol Airport, just a mile or so to the south.

The Schipholdijk is one of dozens of channels built to drain the polder land on which the airport now stands. Until the land was reclaimed in 1852, this shallow, stormy inland sea was notorious for shipwrecks – hence its name, which means 'ship's hell'. Later, it was the site of Fort Schiphol, one of a ring of more than 50 fortified outposts built between 1880 and 1914. The Netherlands stayed neutral during World War I, so it never saw action; by the time World War II broke out, it was obsolete. The surviving forts are now a UNESCO World Heritage site.

5 Continue down the Schipholdijk for about 400yd (366m). Immediately in front of you, a major ring road, the A9, cuts the park in two. Just before you reach it, turn left at an angle and follow the path for about 100yd (91m). On your left is a small lake with an island.

The Vogeleiland (Bird Island) and the margins of its lake form a botanical garden which protects many of the rarer native plants found in the Amsterdamse Bos, including several rare orchids.

6 With the lake on your left, the path meets a crossroads with a small wooden footbridge crossing the narrow stream in front of you. Do not cross this, but turn right, on a slightly wider footpath curving eastward, following the stream. At the next small footbridge, cross the stream into the farmyard of the Geitenboerderij De Ridammerhoeve.

The Ridammerhoeve goat farm is a working farm where you can buy organic cheese, yoghurt and goat's milk products.

7 Leaving the farm, cross the footbridge again and turn left, following the path south-east for around 100yd (91m) to the next stretch of water. This serpentine lake is the Kleine Vijver. Follow its shore for 300yd (274m) to where a narrow channel connects it with a larger lake, the Grote Vijver. Turn right to cross this channel by the footbridge and stroll north-east along a curving path for about 100yd (91m) to return to the park entrance. Walk about 350yd (320m) east to the bus stop, to return to central Amsterdam.

Say Cheese:
A Stroll Around Edam

The former fishing town of Edam is now famous for a completely different export – and it's a great day out from Amsterdam.

Edam is only a couple of miles from the shore of the Zuider Zee, but it has turned its back resolutely on maritime life in favour of farming. The export for which it is famous all over the world is made from the milk of cows that graze in the lush pastures nearby, and sealed in a distinctive coating of red wax. Edam sees far fewer tourists than Amsterdam (except during the high summer 'cheese season') and, although at its best in summer, this neat little town with its rows of tidy brick houses capped by crow-step gables is a very pleasant place for a stroll at any time. Nearby Volendam (just 2 miles/3.2km away) is a former fishing harbour that a century ago attracted painters including Pablo Picasso. But the completion of the dyke that sealed off the Zuider Zee in 1932 ended the fishing trade and today it rests on its tourism laurels. Its postcard-pretty streets are crammed with souvenir shops, and yachts and leisure cruisers have taken the place of fishing smacks.

Catch bus 110 or 118 from Amsterdam Centraal; twice hourly, journey time around 35 minutes. Leave Edam bus station by the east exit; turn left, then, without crossing the water of the Nieuwe Haven, turn immediately right on Schepenmakersdijk and walk one block eastward along this canalside street with the water on your left.

As its name implies, this was once the heart of a boat-building industry that flourished from the 17th century until the silting-up of the Zuider Zee's harbours killed their trade. In plain view ahead of you is a white-painted swing bridge. This is the Kwakelbrug, one of the oldest bridges in the Netherlands (it appears on Johan Blaeu's famous 17th-century map of Edam). Pause as you cross it to look to your right (east), to where a narrow canal joins the broader Nieuwe Haven at a sharp right angle. This stretch of water is still called the *boeren verdriet* (farmer's lament) because produce barges so often ran aground while trying to negotiate it.

2 Ahead (only 200yd/183m away) is an obvious landmark – the medieval tower of the Speeltoren. Cross the bridge and continue straight on along Kwakelsteeg for one block; turn right then almost immediately sharp left on Lingerzijde and follow this main road, keeping to the right, for two blocks, past Molenweg on your left. Lingerzijde merges into Kleine Kerkestraat just before it takes a sharp right. The church is at the corner, on your right.

The graceful, late Gothic bell-tower is the only surviving part of a church that stood here from around 1350 until the late 19th century. The tower, built in the 16th century, was spared when the nave of the church was demolished in 1882 after many years of neglect.

3 Cross Kleine Kerkestraat to the side opposite the church and turn left up Kapsteeg. Walk one short block, cross Graaf Willemstraat, and walk one even shorter block to Bierkade (where the town's beer supply was traditionally unloaded from brewery barges). Turn right here, then almost immediately left into the Kaasmarkt.

On your left is the brightly painted Kaaswaag (Cheese Weigh-house), built in 1778. Edam received the right from the Emperor Charles V (then ruler of the Low Countries) to have a market, which was held every week continuously until 1922. Farmers brought their cheese into town by cart or canal boat, and it was unloaded and hauled to the market square by members of the cheese-porters

133

DISTANCE **2 miles (3.2km)**

ALLOW **half a day**

START **Edam bus station, Singelweg**

FINISH **Edam bus station, Singelweg**

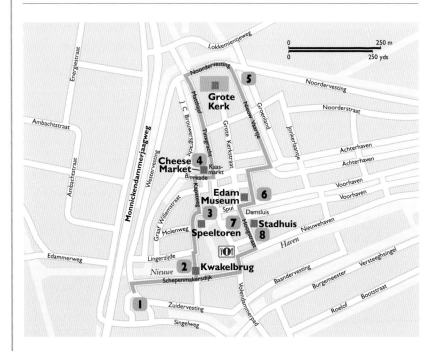

guild. You can still see these guys in action in their traditional white outfits, neckerchiefs and straw boaters, at the cheese market that is held every summer – though it's now a tourist spectacle rather than the real thing. Edam cheese doesn't have EU Place of Origin status, so it can be made anywhere. Now in fact more is made in Germany and Denmark than in the Netherlands.

CHEESE MARKET;

JUL-AUG WED 10.30-12.30

www.edammerkaasmarkt.nl

4 Keeping the Kaaswaag on your left, walk to the north of the Kaasmarkt, turn briefly left then right onto Matthijs Tinxgracht and walk along the narrow canal for two blocks. The Grote Kerk, standing in its own gardens, is on the right, where Matthus Tinxgracht meets two wider canals, Westervesting and Noordervesting. Don't cross the bridge, but turn right to enter the Grote Kerk.

You may think this church looks remarkably sprightly for its age. Built

in the early 15th century, it is dedicated to St Nicholas. Like almost all medieval churches, it has been expanded and altered over centuries; following a severe fire in 1602 it had to be almost completely rebuilt, with the addition of 31 lovely stained-glass windows.

Further work to repair the ravages of time began in 1962 and was completed only in 1979, when the church was reconsecrated – hence its excellent state of preservation.

GROTE KERK;

DAILY APR-OCT 2-4.30 www.vvv-edam.nl

5 Leave the church and, with the water of the Noordervesting on your left, walk clockwise round the church to take the first right into Nieuw Vaartje. With the water of the Nieuw Vaartje on your left, walk two long blocks and one very short block, to where this canal meets the Achterhaven to your left. At the very end of Nieuw Vaartje, turn right on Eilandsgracht then immediately left on Breestraat for two short blocks, and turn right on the north bank of the Voorhaven. To your left, across the street, a solid brick bridge

ABOVE: CHILDREN CARRYING EDAM CHEESES

crosses the Voorhaven, and on your right is the Edam Museum.

This pretty, four-storey building in red brick, with white stone embellishments, crow-stepped gables and red wooden shutters is the oldest brick building in Edam. It was built around 1530, and it's an attractively lop-sided construction that has been added to by various owners over the centuries. Inside, you get a rare glimpse of what holds these seemingly rickety old buildings together – a massive framework of black oak beams, corbels and cross-pieces. The so-called floating cellar was a feature of houses like these – a space designed to contain flooding and keep the rooms above ground dry.

EDAM MUSEUM;
APR-OCT TUE-SAT 10-4.30, SUN 1.30-4.30
www.vvv-edam.nl

6 Turn left out of the door of the museum, then immediately right across the substantial arched bridge, the Damsluis.

Unlike the low wooden swing-bridges or drawbridges that cross so many Dutch canals and can be hauled up to allow vessels to pass through, the Damsluis is a massive permanent fixture. It was not built primarily as a crossing, but as a flood barrier to prevent the waters of the nearby Markermeer inundating the streets of Edam. Most citizens must have welcomed it, but it incurred the wrath of the town's shipbuilders because it blocked the way to the sea for their vessels. They made several attempts to sabotage work

on the new bridge, but were finally forced to accept it.

7 On the other side of the bridge is the Damplein, Edam's miniature main square. Cross the square to the entrance of the imposing Stadhuis, which faces you as you cross.

Edam's Town Hall, dating from the 18th century, shows that the city had a high opinion of itself. Edam's coat of arms – a black cow surmounted by three gold stars on a red shield – is above the entrance. Upstairs is an annex of the Edam Museum that is dedicated to, among other things, three local people of extremes. Pride of place goes to Trijntje Keever. Poor Trijntje, born in 1616, shot up to a height of almost 9ft (2.7m) before her early death at the age of 17. A pair of her size-55 shoes is displayed with her portrait. Also pictured are two 17th-century figures: Jan Claaesenz, a local landlord who weighed a colossal 455lb (206kg); and a former mayor of Edam, Pieter Dirckz, who managed to grow his beard to a length of almost 7ft (2.1m)

STADHUIS;
APR-OCT TUE-SAT 10-4.30, SUN 1.30-4.30
www.vvv-edam.nl

8 Turn left from the museum doorway, left again and, from the south-west corner of Damplein, walk two very short blocks to Nieuwe Haven. Turn right, turn left across the canal at the next bridge, then right again, passing the Kwakelbrug, to retrace your steps to the bus station.

The Heart
of Haarlem

**Haarlem has the best of medieval Amsterdam. Discover almshouses,
an apothecary's garden and a church where Mozart performed.**

Only 16 miles (25.7km) and less than 25 minutes by train from central
Amsterdam, Haarlem is in many ways closer to most people's idea of Amsterdam
than Amsterdam itself: it has the pretty medieval houses, churches and canals
without the sleaze, drugs and commercialism that beset Amsterdam's tourist
ghettoes. Visit in spring or early summer and your journey will take you through
miles of fields swathed in the vivid reds and yellows of tulips and daffodils.
Haarlem feels like Amsterdam in miniature. Like its bigger neighbour, it
flourished in the 17th century and was built on manmade islands dredged from
concentric rings of canals. Its glory days came after the Netherlands finally won
independence from Spain, and many of its landmark buildings are the work of
Protestant master masons who fled from Spanish-occupied Flanders to re-settle
in the free United Provinces. By the 1620s, more than half of Haarlem's residents
were emigrants from the south. These were not penniless refugees. Many were
wealthy, well connected and involved in international commerce.

Amsterdam Centraal Station; between 3-6 departures an hour, journey time 15-25 minutes. Leave Haarlem's railway station by the main exit and cross Stationsplein.

Look back at the station's grand façade. Like Amsterdam Centraal or the great rail termini of London, it's a product of the great days of steam, when stations were built to look like palaces.

2 From the south-west corner of Stationsplein, follow the lefthand side of Kruisweg past the bus station on your left across Parklaan and the water of the Nieuwe Gracht, and continue down Kruisstraat to Haarlem's centre.

Master-builder Lieven de Key (1560-1627) was one of the Flemings lured to Haarlem in the aftermath of the Spanish wars (another was his near-contemporary, the painter Frans Hals, who features in Walk 21), and the heart of the city is very much his creation. Old Haarlem's heart is reminiscent of medieval Bruges or Ghent – as if de Key and his sponsors were trying to recreate their southern homes here in the north.

3 Carry on along Kruisstraat. Just before the southern end of Kruisstraat, where it merges with Barteljorisstraat, take a quick peek to your right, through an amazing wrought-iron gate and an elaborate rococo entrance, into the concealed courtyard of the Hofje van Oorschot at Kruisstraat 44.

WHERE TO EAT
(For more choices see Walk 21)

🍴 MA BROWN'S,
Nieuwe Groenmarkt 31;
Tel: 023 531 5829.
www.mabrownsrestaurant.nl
British owner-chef Mike Cowley serves what he likes to describe as 'English cuisine for modern tastes'. Open for lunch and afternoon tea only. €€

🍴 BAKEMA & CO,
Oude Groenmarkt 24;
Tel: 023 532 8322.
www.bakemaenco.nl
Stylish restaurant with a French twist, open for lunch and dinner, with an attractive terrace. €

Haarlem's historic *hofjes* are almshouses built around a small central garden, usually prettily laid out with shrubs and flower beds and sometimes having a central fountain or water pump. They were often endowed by wealthy individuals or groups of well-off philanthropists and became home to elderly widows and widowers who had no family to care for or support them financially. Hofje van Oorschot is one of the grander Haarlem almshouses. Wouterus van Oorschot (1704-68) bequeathed a legacy to build it. It has two wings – each comprising eight little houses – either side of a main building that originally housed communal areas and caretakers' offices. Between the

20

DISTANCE **3 miles (4.8km)**

ALLOW **3 hours**

START **Haarlem Stationsplein**

FINISH **Haarlem Stationsplein**

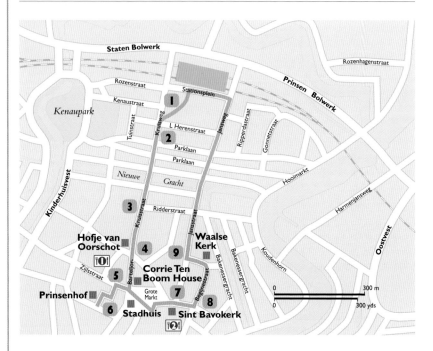

buildings is a lush green shared garden. The site was originally the home of the Heilige Geesthuis (House of the Holy Spirit), a religious foundation dating from the 14th century. After the Reformation, this Catholic community was dissolved and the building became an orphanage. Visitors are welcome to wander in the peaceful courtyard during daylight hours, but are respectfully requested not to make any noise.

HOFJE VAN OORSCHOT;
DAILY 10-5 www.vvvzk.nl

4 At the end of Kruisstraat, cross the street and continue down what is now Barteljorisstraat. Keep to the lefthand (east) side of the street for its entire one-block length. At No. 19 turn left to enter the fascinating Corrie Ten Boom House.

The Ten Boom family were devout Christians who sheltered Jews and Resistance members during the German occupation of World War II. On 28 February 1944, the house was raided and

the Ten Booms were arrested. Corrie's father, sister and two brothers died in Ravensbruck concentration camps, but Corrie survived, after being released by mistake in December 1944. She later told her story in her book *The Hiding Place* (filmed in 1975), and in 1988 the family home became a museum. When they came for the Ten Booms, the Gestapo missed a tiny concealed apartment where four Jewish refugees and two Resistance fighters were hidden. They escaped after the raid. Corrie Ten Boom died on 15 April 1983 on her 91st birthday.

CORRIE TEN BOOM HOUSE;
APR-OCT TUE-SAT 10-3.30, NOV-MAR TUE-SAT 11-2.30 www.corrietenboom.com

5 Carry on the full length of the block, turn right on Zijlsstraat, cross the street and almost immediately turn left into 't Pand, a small alley which jinks almost immediately left, then right, to a stone gateway that opens into the Prinsenhof.

This pretty square planted with flowers and herbs was first laid out in 1721 as an apothecary's garden of medicinal plants. In the centre of the square stands a statue of one of Haarlem's native sons, the printer Laurens Janszoon Coster (1370–1440). He was an important man in 15th-century Haarlem, serving as sexton of the nearby Sint-Bavokerk and as town treasurer. He may also have invented printing using moveable type almost a decade before the German, Johann Gutenberg, who usually gets all the credit. After Coster's death, his apprentice Johann Fust is said to have sneaked off with Coster's presses and type to Mainz, where he went into partnership with Gutenberg.

6 Retrace your steps to Zijlsstraat, turn right, and walk less than 50yd (46m) to the corner of Zijlsstraat and Grote Markt, Haarlem's medieval main square, which still looks very much as it did when Frans Hals painted it in the

17th century. Turn right at the corner and almost immediately turn right again to enter the Stadhuis.

The dramatic façade dates from 1633, when it was rebuilt by the city architect, Lieven de Key, who also added a north wing (at the corner of Zijlsstraat) and a grand staircase leading to the Count's Hall within. Five coloured pillars outside the Stadhuis are a modern memorial to de Key, created by the sculptor Roger Raveel in 1990. Above the main entrance stands an allegorical figure representing Justice, with a drawn sword in her right hand and a set of scales in her left. This is also de Key's work.

The oldest parts of Haarlem's town hall date from the 14th century, when it was a hunting lodge owned by the Counts of Holland. Count William V added the Count's Hall, which is decorated with portraits of counts and countesses and with a graphically gruesome portrait of the Grim Reaper, intended to remind them that all good things must come to an end.

7 Now cross Grote Markt (passing another statue of Laurens Janszoon Coster in the centre of the square) to the south-east corner and the great Gothic church, Sint-Bavokerk.

The church was built between 1370 and 1520; its transept was designed by the Flemish master builder Evert Spowater of Antwerp, and the ubiquitous de Key modernized its Renaissance font chapel in 1593. In contrast to many Dutch churches, the interior is light and airy. It is dominated by one of the world's largest organs, with 5,000 pipes and 64 registers. Mozart played here during his tour of the Netherlands in 1766.

8 Leaving the Sint-Bavokerk (also known as the Grote Kerk), turn right on Grote Kerk Lange, then turn almost immediately left in front of the grand 19th-century Concertgebouw, considered one of the finest in Europe, onto Begijnestraat. Walk north on the righthand side for two blocks, then turn right into the Begijnhof.

Within the courtyard is the Waalse Kerk (or Walloon Church). This medieval church was a place of prayer first for French-speaking expatriates from the southern provinces of the Low Countries (now part of Belgium). After the Reformation and Dutch independence it was taken over by Protestant Huguenots who had been exiled from Catholic France. The façade, with its attractive doorway festooned with sculpted flowers, fruit and foliage, is much later than the original church, and dates from 1670.

9 Turn left at the north end of Begijnhof, then turn right onto Jansstraat; walk to the end of the street and cross the Nieuwe Gracht and Parklaan via Jansweg to return to the station. Alternatively, you can combine this walk with Walk 21, Art and Antiquities in Harlaam, by turning right at the north end of the Begijnhof, then right again at the Bakenessergracht.

143

VIEW OF THE SPAARNE RIVER WITH GRAVESTENENBRUG DRAWBRIDGE IN HAARLEM

Art and Antiquities in Haarlem

Follow Haarlem's ancient waterways on a walk that leads past a fortified 14th-century gateway and takes in a collection of Frans Hals's paintings.

Haarlem's fortunes were built on its weaving and spinning industries. Founded in 1245, by the 15th century it was a wealthy cloth-making centre. It suffered, however, during the Wars of Independence, when it was besieged and sacked by the Spaniards in 1572-3, then partially destroyed by fire in 1576. Prosperity returned during the post-independence Golden Age of the 17th century, when it became once again one of the richest cities in the Netherlands. This walk takes you along the banks of some of Haarlem's waterways, from the narrow Bakenessergracht to the banks of the serpentine River Spaarne, which meanders its way through the city centre and once formed part of the boundaries of medieval Haarlem. Pause on the way to visit a museum dedicated to one of the most famous of Dutch painters, before ending on a delightful main square that keeps much of its original architecture and is conveniently packed with cafés and restaurants. Haarlem is a compact town, and you can easily combine this walk with Walk 20 for a full day out – and still have plenty of time for lunch.

I Amsterdam Centraal Station; between 3-6 departures an hour, journey time 15-25 minutes. Leaving the station, turn left to leave Stationsplein; turn right on Jansweg, cross Parklaan and Nieuwe Gracht. Walk one block down Jansstraat; turn left on Korte Jansstraat then almost immediately right onto the west bank of Bakenessergracht. This little canal is lined with some of the oldest houses in Haarlem. Turn right at the end of the first short block on Bakenessergracht, into Goudsmitspleintje, and turn to face the dignified building which faces south onto the small square.

Goudsmitspleintje – as its name suggests – was the home of Haarlem's workers in precious metals. This was their guild house and above its doorway is a gablestone that bears a carved chalice and the words *Dit is de Goud Smits Cammer* (This is the Goldsmiths Chamber).

2 Turn about, walk back to the canalside and turn right, then left, to cross the canal by the Begijnebrug. Now turn right and walk down one block with the canal on your right. The tower of the Bakenesser Kerk is a prominent landmark ahead and to your left; at Vrouwstraat, turn left and walk one very short block. The church is on your right.

This 15th-century church is one of the most impressive buildings in Haarlem. Unlike most Dutch churches, its steeple is stone, not lead-covered wood, giving its 26-bell carillon an especially rich note. The tower was originally destined for Haarlem's Grote Kerk but was found to be too heavy, so this church – also called Onze Lieve Vrouwe – was specially built to make use of it. The church is open by appointment only; Johannes Bosboom's painting of the interior, showing the church as it was in the 17th century but dating from around 1860, can be seen in the Amsterdams Historisch Museum.

3 Continue to the end of Vrouwstraat with the north wall of the church on your right. At the corner, turn right on Het Krom, walk past the front of the Bakenesser Kerk, and carry on down the lefthand side of Het Krom for a further block until you reach the water of the Binnenspaarne or Inner Spaarne. The river is lined on both sides with picturesque 17th- and 18th-century brick houses, three to four storeys high. Many are capped with decorative gables in a variety of styles. Cross the street to the waterside, turn right and walk along the river bank for one block to the Wildemansbrug to recross the Bakenessergracht where it meets the river. On your left as soon as you reach the opposite bank is a picturesque white-framed drawbridge, the Gravenstenebrug.

Pause for a moment to admire the stylish twin façades of the former Oliphant Brewery, opposite, with their contrasting red and white brick and stonework and crow-step gables. In the 17th century there were more than 50 breweries along the banks of the Spaarne, which provided a plentiful supply of water for brewing

147

21

DISTANCE **3.5 miles (5.6km)**

ALLOW **3-4 hours**

START **Haarlem Stationsplein**

FINISH **Haarlem Grote Markt**

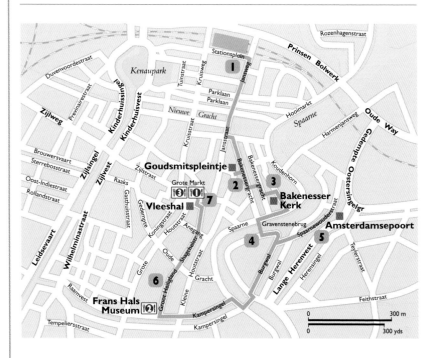

and a means of transporting barrels
of beer by barge. The former brewery
is now in the care of the Vereniging
Hendrick de Keyser, the leading Dutch
architectural heritage association.

4 Cross the Gravenstenebrug, turn
left on Koorte Spaarne and follow
the river bank; after one block, the
street jogs right at the mouth of the
narrow Burgwaalspaarne where it joins
the river. Cross this narrow waterway
and from the end of the bridge, follow

the lefthand side of Spaarnewouderstraat
for two long blocks, passing Sleutelstraat,
then Koralesteeg on your left, until you
reach Melkbouwsteeg. Cross the road.
The red-brick Amsterdamsepoort, with
its arched gateway, towers and grey
pointed turrets, is right in front of you,
straddling the water of the Herensingel.

This is the only survivor from a ring of
12 fortified gateways that defended the
city, built in 1355. It was a key point in
the defence of Haarlem during the siege

of 1573, when the city held out against the Spanish troops of the Duke of Toledo for seven months. When the city finally surrendered, the Spaniards massacred most of its people, drowning many of them by throwing them into the Spaarne, tied together in pairs.

5 Face about and retrace your steps to the Burgwaalspaarne. The name of this small waterway indicates that it once followed the line of the city walls and formed part of Haarlem's defences. Recross the bridge, and turn left along the waterside, where houseboats, yachts and leisure cruisers are moored. With the canal on your left, keep going for two longish blocks, all the way to the point where Burgwaalspaarne meets the Spaarne again. On reaching the end of Burgwaalspaarne, cross Antoniestraat and take the Lieve Vrouwegracht bridge across the river. At the west end of the bridge, cross the busy main road, turn right and cross another wide and busy bridge to the north side of the Kampersingel. This is the easternmost of three canals that run into each other, forming a belt that marks the southern boundary of the old city. Follow its waterside for four blocks, then cross Groot Heiligland, turn right and less than halfway up the block, turn left into the Frans Hals Museum at No. 62.

The imposing complex of 17th-century buildings that houses the museum was originally a *hofje*, designed by Lieven de Key (1560-1627) during his tenure as city architect. It later became an orphanage,

WHERE TO EAT

🍽 QUATRE MAINS,
Grote Markt 4;
Tel: 023 542 4258.
Small, friendly and affordable spot on Haarlem's historic square, specializing in fondues but with some fish and meat alternatives. €

🍽 FRANS HALS MUSEUM,
Groot Heiligland 62;
Tel: 023 511 5815.
The light and spacious museum café serves snacks, light meals, cakes, tea, coffee and soft drinks. €

🍽 JILL'S,
Grote Markt 10;
Tel: 023 532 9424.
www.jills.nl
Mediterranean-influenced set menus and à la carte meals. A place for a full meal at the end of your walk rather than a midway snack. (€€-€€€)

then in 1906 it was bought by the municipality. Two new wings were added, the older parts were modernized, and the 17th-century garden and courtyard were restored. Antwerp-born Hals came to Haarlem aged 10, in 1581. Like his contemporary Rembrandt, he made a bundle during the boom years of the 17th century, painting portraits of well-off Haarlem burghers and city militia companies in a newly realistic style. Credited with fathering modern painting, Hals fathered numerous illegitimate

children, as well as a brood of 10 legitimate sons and daughters, and he had a powerful thirst as well. By 1664, aged 79 he was broke. Saved from penury by a pension from the town council, he died two years later. The museum has more than 20 of his paintings, as well as works by some of his illustrious contemporaries.

FRANS HALS MUSEUM;

TUE-SAT 11-5, SUN 12-5

www.franshalsmuseum.com

6 Turn left out of the museum and follow Groot Heiligland for three short blocks to Gedempte Oude Gracht. Cross this, and continue up Shagchelstraat to Anegang. Cross again, to enter Warmoesstraat, a smart shopping street lined with art and antique shops, which opens onto the wide Grote Markt. Turn immediately left, then left again, to enter a huge building with an elaborate red-brick, gabled front.

ABOVE: BANQUET OF THE OFFICERS OF THE ST GEORGE MILITIA COMPANY, FRANS HALS

The Vleeshal, formerly the meat market hall, is a superb piece of Dutch Renaissance architecture, built in 1603 when the city was emerging from the traumatic years of the revolt against Spain. It now forms the core of De Hallen, an annex of the Frans Hals Museum, with a collection of 20th and 21st century art. More recently, the collection has been broadened to include work by non-Dutch painters and photographers,

including contemporary British artists Tracey Emin and Sarah Lucas.

DE HALLEN;
TUE-SAT 11-5, SUN 12-5
www.franshalsmuseum.com

7 This walk ends on the Grote Markt. To make a beeline back to Centraal Station, cross the square to the north-east corner and follow Janstraat, then Jansweg, to Stationsplein.

Utrecht:
The Oldest City

Climb the tallest church tower in the Netherlands for the best view of Utrecht's medieval legacy, marred in some places by modern building.

Utrecht bases its claim to be the Netherlands' oldest city on evidence that the Romans built a settlement here as early as 48AD, although they felt little need to conquer the sparsely peopled salt marshes of the region they called Batavia. During the Dark Ages, Friesians and Franks built wooden forts here, and in the late 7th century St Willibrord (658-739) and 12 Benedictine monks founded a community. Willibrord and his followers came from Northumbria, which had only recently become exposed to Christianity, and were keen to spread the gospel to their Friesian cousins. They were remarkably successful (though the Duke of Friesia refused to convert, saying that he would rather go to hell with his pagan ancestors than to heaven without them). Under the protection of the Frankish ruler Pepin II, Utrecht became a bishop's see in 696. Willibrord became its first archbishop and converted most of the northern Netherlands to Christianity. Utrecht's city status dates from its charter of 1122. For centuries it was the wealthiest and most powerful city in the northern Low Countries.

Trains for Utrecht leave from Amsterdam Centraal Station at least twice hourly, journey time is about 30 minutes. Leave Utrecht Centraal Station by the east exit; turn right and walk along Stationsplein with the station on your right, then turn left to cross the Moreelsepark gardens. The immediate view from Stationsplein is unpromising, as the opposite side of the square is entirely occupied by the vast modern Hoog Catharijne shopping centre. Persevere; once you have crossed the busy Catharijnebaan into Mariaplaats, a more interesting prospect emerges, with the 367ft (112m) Domtoren looming almost dead ahead. At the end of Mariaplaats, take a dogleg right (on Mariastraat), then immediately left onto Zadelstraat for one short block. Turn left onto Donkerstraat, keeping on the righthand side of the street, then turn right into Buurkersteeg and the Buurkerkhof courtyard.

Look up at the façade of this former church where the buurs or common people worshipped. To the left and high up, two cannonballs embedded in the stonework are claimed to be relics of the Spanish bombardment of the city in 1572. Walk around the church to the right to enter what is now the Nationaal Museum van Speelklok tot Pierement. Inside is a collection of every kind of mechanical musical instrument – the museum's name means 'from musical clock to barrel organ' and it lives up to its name, with a charming collection of clocks, bells and pianolas.

WHERE TO EAT

🍽 SIRTAKI,
Sevetstraat 1;
Tel: 030 232 8316.
Friendly Greek restaurant near Domplein serving favourites such as moussaka, dolmades, souvlaki and salads. €€

🍽 BROERS STADSCAFE,
Janskerkhof 9;
Tel: 020 234 3406.
Cheap and fairly basic café near the Domplein. €

🍽 STATIONSRESTAURATIE DE TIJD,
Stationshal 8,
Utrecht Centraal Station;
Tel: 030 230 4211.
The main selling point of this café-restaurant is its convenient location. The food isn't outstanding. €

NATIONAAL MUSEUM VAN SPEELKLOK TOT PIEREMENT;
TUE-SUN 10-5 www.museumspeelklok.nl

2 On the north side of the church courtyard turn right on Steenweg. After just a few steps, at the end of Steenweg cross Choorweg and the Zoutmarkt to the Oude Gracht canal; cross the bridge ahead of you, turn right on Vismarkt then left on Servetstraat for one block. You are now on the tree-shaded Domplein, with the Domtoren looming above you on your right.

153

DISTANCE 4.5 miles (7.2km)

ALLOW 4 hours

START Utrecht Centraal Station

FINISH Utrecht Centraal Station

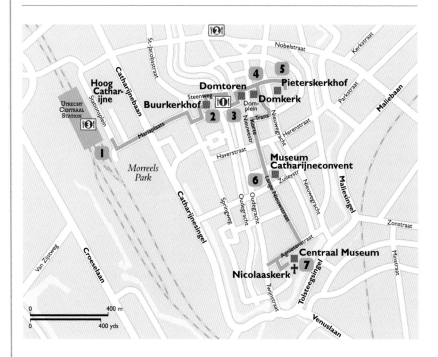

Take a deep breath before you climb because the 14th-century Domtoren is the tallest church tower in the Netherlands. To reach its highest gallery you must climb 456 steps. Take a breather midway in the belfry, a mere 165ft (50m) up, to look at its great bells, which weigh 34 tons in total. The bells peal out a different tune each 15 minutes.

3 Descend the tower and cross the Domplein to the Domkerk on its south side.

The Domtoren's carillon has 13 bells. In view of the church's unlucky history, you may think this is tempting fate. The two parts of the building were originally connected by a vast nave, which occupied what is now the Domplein and was destroyed by a great storm in 1674. The church was begun in 1254 (on the site of an earlier Romanesque cathedral that burned down in the previous year), but was not completed until 1520. Soon after, the ferment of the Protestant Reformation stripped it of its ornate

Catholic interior. Inside the Domkerk's austere interior, only the north and south transepts and two chapels remain.

The statue in the centre of the Domplein is of John, Count of Nassau, brother of the leader of the revolt against Spain, William the Silent, Prince of Orange. The Union of Utrecht, signed here in 1579, created the United Provinces, the state which eventually became the Netherlands, so it has the same historic resonance for the Dutch as the Declaration of Independence for America.

In front of the Domkerk a huge runestone bearing the date 980 AD was a gift to the city from the people of Denmark, commemorating the conversion of the Danes to Christianity by holy monks from Utrecht – thus completing a task that St Willibrord had begun by leading a mission to the Danes almost 300 years earlier.

4 Leave the church. Turn right out of the door, right on the north side of Domplein, cross Achter de Dom and walk east on Voetiusstraat for one block, crossing Nieuwegracht. Staying on the righthand side, take the next right into Pieterskerkhof.

Built in 1048, the Romanesque Pieterskerkhof is an impressive sight. The oldest church in Utrecht, it is also among the oldest in northern Europe, and the body of Bishop Bernold, who died six years after seeing his great church completed, is entombed in the crypt. By Bernold's time, the Bishops of Utrecht were far from being gentle missionaries, whose only aim was to spread the gospel and do God's work. They had become worldly feudal princes, answerable only to the Pope and the Holy Roman Empire and holding sway even over the Counts of Holland.

ABOVE: GARGOYLE ON THE DOMKERK

5 Retrace your steps to the corner of Voetiusstraat and Achter de Dom, cross Achter de Dom and turn left. Walk one block down Achter de Dom and turn right on Trans. Follow this for one block. Turn left on Korte Nieuwstraat. After one block, this becomes Lange Nieuwstraat. Stay walking on the lefthand side for three blocks. At the end of the third block, Catharijnesteeg is on your left. Cross this narrow street, and just after crossing, at Lange Nieuwstraat 38, turn left into the Museum Catharijneconvent.

For English speakers, the name is confusing. This was never a convent, but a monastery built for the Knights Hospitaller of the Order of St John around 1560. The order was founded in 1113, after the First Crusade, to administer medical aid to pilgrims and crusaders in the Holy Land. The red eight-pointed cross of the order has since become universally known as the Maltese Cross. The green version still symbolizes medical care in most European countries.

The Catharijnhof is now a most ecumenical museum, dedicated to intelligent examination of the turbulent religious history of the Netherlands. The lavish gold and silver ornaments, elaborately jewelled crucifixes and caskets, sculptures and ornately penned manuscripts displayed within the former cloisters are reminders that before the Protestant Reformation the great churches of the Netherlands were not the relatively austere places of worship that they are today.

MUSEUM CATHARIJNECONVENT;
TUE-FRI 10-5, SAT-SUN 11-5
www.catharijneconvent.nl

6 Turn left on leaving the convent and continue down Lange Nieuwstraat for four blocks, to the end of the street and the junction with Agnietenstraat. Turn right on Agnietenstraat, cross the street and after one long block take the first left into Nicolaaskerkhof, then follow it round to your right. The Centraal Museum administration office is on your left as you turn off Agnietenstraat – don't confuse this with the entrance to the museum itself, which is located just round the corner, on your right, at No. 10.

Portraits by Jan van Scorel (1495-1562), the Utrecht-born painter known (if only by his fellow-citizens) as the Dutch Leonardo, have pride of place here in a room of their own on the museum's mezzanine floor. Van Scorel brought back the concept of the group portrait from a visit to Renaissance Rome. It quickly gained popularity in the Netherlands and made the fortunes of rival painters such as Rembrandt and Hals, whose portraits of militia companies are much better known than van Scorel's work.

CENTRAAL MUSEUM;
SUN-THU 12-5 FRI 12-9
www.centraalmuseum.nl

7 Return to Agnietenstraat, cross the street and turn left to the bus stop midway along the block. Bus 2 takes you back to Stationsplein.

A TYPICAL DUTCH SCENE OF BIKES AND BRIDGES

In Rembrandt's Footsteps in Leiden

Discover Rembrandt's early life in Leiden, from the sights he saw as a child, to the university at which he enrolled precociously early.

Amsterdam gets most of Rembrandt's reflected glory, even though the city wasn't all that kind to him in the end. But he was born and raised in Leiden, and it was in this city of scholars and artisans that he learned his trade, created his first masterpieces, and was inspired by the histories of ancient Rome, the myths of Classical Greece, and the stories of the Old and New Testaments. Leiden was already a centre of learning in Rembrandt's time and the seat of the oldest university in the Netherlands, but it was also a place of hard-headed merchants – some of whom became the young painter's first clients – and hard-working artisans, like his mill-owning grandfather, father and brothers. Strangely, Leiden makes less of Rembrandt van Rijn than does Amsterdam. A small bridge, a riverside park, and a drab street were named after him more than 250 years after his death, but for those who care to explore there are plenty of places associated with him as a young man. Leiden is a compact city, on the east bank of the River Rhine, from which, of course, Rembrandt took his surname.

Amsterdam Centraal Station; 5-6 trains an hour, journey time around 30 minutes. Leave Leiden station by the main (south) exit and cross to the south side of Stationsplein, to the corner of Stationsplein and Stationsweg. Turn right, walk one block to the traffic roundabout at the end of Stationsplein. Turn left here (anti-clockwise). Cross Morssingel, the first exit from the roundabout, and take the second exit, Morssweg, with the greenery of the Morssingelpark on your left. At the south end of the park, Morssweg curves sharply right, and here you turn left onto Morsstraat. Cross the street to the south side, turn left, then immediately right. Your first landmark is impossible to miss: it's the Put Windmill, standing where the Rhine meets the Galgewater canal.

The mill is a faithful copy (built in 1987) of the windmill erected here by Jan Janszoon Put in 1669. Put had permission from the town council to move the mill from its original site, east of the town centre. Windmills were not permanent structures – their wooden towers, sails and machinery could easily be dismantled and reassembled on a new site. When this mill was rebuilt here, Rembrandt was 12 years old and his home was just on the other side of the Galgewater, so you can imagine him watching the reconstruction work with interest.

2 Leaving the windmill behind and on your right, cross the canalside street, Kort Galgewater, and the Rembrandtbrug, a white-framed

swing-bridge, to the other side of the canal, and walk across a small square – the Schildersplaats – towards the Rhine, then follow Galgewater as it curves sharply to the left.

Rembrandt's family lived on the Weddesteeg, just within the city walls on the south bank of the Galgewater, for several generations. His grandfather, aunt and great aunt all had homes here, and Rembrandt lived here with his parents for the first 25 years of his life, from 15 July 1606 until 1631, but there is now no trace of the family home.

3 On your right is a small patch of riverside urban greenery, the Rembrandtpark. Walk past this and cross the next main street you come to, Noordeinde.

Rembrandt's family owned several windmills in this part of Leiden. His maternal grandfather, Gerrit Roelefzoon, had a mill a few hundred yards away, on the right bank of the Rhine; when this was destroyed by Spanish marauders during the siege of 1573, Gerrit built a new mill on the town wall above the Weddesteeg. Later, Rembrandt's brother built a mill south of Noordeinde.

4 On the south side of Noordeinde, walk through a pedestrian underpass between the Boerhaave School, which stands on the site of the mill owned by Rembrandt's brother, and walk down the righthand side of Witte Singel, with the canal on your right.

161

DISTANCE 4 miles (6.4km)

ALLOW 2.5 hours

START Stationsplein, Leiden

FINISH Stationsplein, Leiden

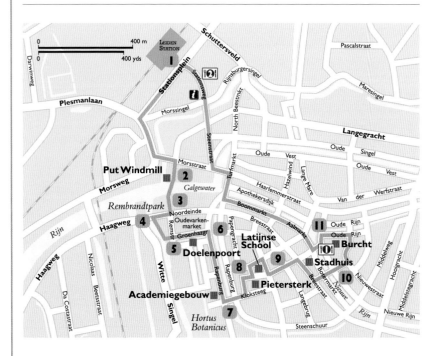

A bust of Rembrandt, by the sculptor Toon Dupui (1877-1937), stands beside the canal, midway down the block. In 1630, Rembrandt bought one of the small kitchen gardens on the river bank here for the not inconsiderable sum of 500 guilders, so he must by that time have been making a fair living from his works of art.

5 At the end of the block, turn left and follow Groenhazengracht, crossing the dull Rembrandtstraat, which

was renamed after the painter in 1879. Walk past the Oudevarkenmarkt, on your left. This was the city's swine market, and you can only begin to imagine how malodorous and noisy it was in Rembrandt's time, with the squealing of pigs and the pong of offal and manure. Ahead of you is the Doelenpoort.

This imposing city gate, topped by a relief of St Joris (St George) despatching the dragon, was built in 1645. It now opens onto the campus of the University of Leiden, but in Rembrandt's time this was an open space, the Doelen, where the Leiden City Guard drilled and practised their musketry skills. All male citizens aged from 18 to 60 years old could be called on to serve as part-time soldiers in this militia, which was also the city's police force. Rembrandt's father, Harmen, served in the guard and was injured by an exploding musket. Thereafter, he paid six guilders a year to the city in lieu of service, until 1617, when one of Rembrandt's brothers took his place in the ranks. Rembrandt seems to have avoided serving, so it is ironic that his most famous painting, *The Night Watch* (see Walk 8), is virtually a recruiting poster for a similar guard company.

6 At the corner of Groenhazengracht and Rapenburg, turn right, keeping the water of the canal on your left. Walk two blocks down this curve of canal with some stately old buildings to either side, and passing on your right, at No. 73, the Academiegebouw, the venerable senate building of Leiden University, built in 1581.

When the precocious Rembrandt enrolled at the university at the early age of 14, he was three or four years younger than his peers, but his student days were shortlived, because he seems already to have been set on a career as a painter. He never actually undertook any studies at the university, and soon left to serve as an apprentice to Jacob von Swanenburgh, a local history painter.

WHERE TO EAT

🍴 **DENDE,**
Nieuwe Rijn 5;
Tel: 071 512 6915.
www.dende.nl
At the time of writing, Dende was the newest and smartest place to eat in Leiden, with an Italian-influenced menu, serving breakfast, snacks, lunch and dinner. €€

🍴 **GRAND CAFÉ LA GARE,**
Stationsweg 7-9;
Tel: 071 512 6120.
French-style café-brasserie conveniently close to the station, good for a drink, snack or lunch when you arrive or while you wait for your train back. €€

7 At the end of Rapenburg, after passing the Academiegebouw, turn left to cross the canal by the Nonnenbrug, which leads to Kloksteeg. Follow this for one short block to Pieterskerkplein, where the Pieterskerk is immediately in front of you. Turn left, then turn right on the north side of the square, then turn right to enter the church.

The Rembrandt family were substantial citizens, so the vault where Rembrandt's mother and father and many of his siblings were buried was prominently placed. However, in the mid-19th century the interior of the church was modernized and those buried within

were re-interred elsewhere. Three now nameless grave slabs lie in front of the pulpit, and one of these was probably the Rembrandt family's tombstone.

8 Exit the church and angle left to turn into a short, narrow lane on your right, the Muskadelsteeg. Follow this to its end and turn right onto Lokhorstraat. Next to the corner and on your right at No. 16 is the entrance to the Latijnse School.

As a young scholar here, Rembrandt studied Latin, Greek and the Old Testament stories which later inspired so many of his paintings. Since he enrolled

early at the university, he may well have been an exceptional pupil.

9 Continue along Lokhorstraat for one short block and take the first right onto Pieterskerkstraat, which leads you back to the north-east corner of the Pieterskerk. Cross to the other side, and enter Pieterskerkchoorsteg, and follow this street for two blocks, crossing Langebrug, where (at No. 89) Rembrandt was apprenticed for three years to Jacob van Swanenburg. Swanenburg had studied painting in Italy, which gave him considerable standing, but the pupil seems quickly to have outgrown the master, whose paintings of

ABOVE: THE RIJINBURGER CANAL BETWEEN STEENSTRAAT AND STATIONSWEG

contemporary Jan Lievens (1607-74), tried jealously to keep a monopoly on art sales in the city, but with limited success. Leiden's wealthy burghers were always interested in new works at bargain prices.

10 Keep the Stadhuis on your left and walk down Breestraat to the corner of Koornbrugsteeg. Turn left here and walk one short block, with the Stadhuisplein on your left (Koornbrugsteeg forms the south side of this square). Cross the narrow channel of the Nieuwe Rijn, and after another short block, turn left at the end of Koornbrugsteeg onto Nieuwestraat. Walk through the gateway at the end of the street into Burchtplein.

Facing you, atop a grassy knoll, are the remnants of a squat stone fort known as the Burcht. Built in the 11th century, it was Leiden's first fortress. From what's left of the ramparts, you have a panoramic view of Amsterdam.

standard religious subjects are best described as competent but uninspired. At the end of Pieterskerkchoorsteg, turn right, cross Breestraat, and turn right again in front of the Stadhuis.

Leiden's grand town hall was severely damaged by fire in 1929, then restored. In Rembrandt's time, it was very much the heart of the city, surrounded by shops and market stalls, and during the annual trade fairs its great hall was used as a commercial art gallery. Rembrandt may have sold some early works here, but he would have had competition from painters from all over the Netherlands. Local painters, including Rembrandt's

11 Walk anti-clockwise around the Burcht, turn left on Oude Rijn, turn left onto the Hoostraat bridge to recross the Nieuwe Rijn, and turn right. With the water on your right, follow Aalmarkt for two fairly long blocks back to Rapenburg. Turn right here, crossing the Galgewater; cross Stille Rijn to your right, then turn immediately left across the Morsstraat bridge, and immediately right on Steenstraat. Follow this for three blocks, crossing the Morssingel, to the south end of Stationsweg and return to Stationsplein and the station.

Leiden:
City of Learning

Leiden, Rembrandt's home town, is also the birthplace of one of Europe's oldest universities and has been a seat of learning for four centuries.

William the Silent, leader of the great Dutch revolt against Spain that lasted for most of the 16th century, endowed Leiden's university in 1575 in recognition of the city's heroic role. Leiden declared for the cause of independence in 1572. The next year it was besieged by the Spaniards and held out for a year, until on 3 October 1574, William broke the siege. His daring seaborne assault involved breaking the dykes to let in the waters of the North Sea, then sailing in to sweep away the surprised Spanish. Leiden soon became a centre of learning and of academic excellence that fostered some astonishing advances in science and philosophy in the 17th and 18th centuries. Leiden's railway station is new, gleaming and gives little hint of the attractive old-fashioned town centre that lies south of the Morssingel canal, which flows into the River Rijn (Rhine) about 400yd (366m) south of the station. This walk will attract those with a taste for the gruesome — a dissecting theatre with a crew of skeletons and a museum stuffed with Egyptian mummies are among its high points.

Trains from Amsterdam Centraal station to Leiden run 5-6 times an hour, journey time about 30 minutes. From the south exit of Leiden station, turn right then left along the side of Stationsplein (the bus station is on the opposite side of the square, on your left). This brings you to Stationsweg. Keep to the left side of the street and walk down about 200yd (183m) to the corner of Morssingel, Stationsweg and Rijnsburgersingel. The VVV city tourist information office is on the corner, on your right, at Stationsweg 2. Cross the road and turn left, keeping the canal on your right, and walk along Rijnsburgersingel for just 200yd (183m) to the Molenwerf bridge. Turn right here, cross the canal and immediately to your right a gate leads into the park that surrounds the Molenmuseum de Valk, which can be seen from the opposite bank all the way from the tourist office.

Leiden's city walls once supported 19 windmills – siting them high up allowed them to catch the breeze more easily. The 90ft (27m) tall de Valk mill is the only survivor, and stands on the site of an earlier mill built in 1611. The introduction of motorized milling in the late 19th century doomed commercial windmills, but de Valk, with four millstones, was one of the largest and went on grinding grain until the mid-20th century. Windmills are of course one of the icons of the Netherlands (along with clogs and tulips) and the museum within offers an insight into the everyday life and work of mill families like

Rembrandt's (see Walk 23). The family home was on the ground floor, where the rooms are furnished exactly as they would have been in the 19th century, with simple wooden furniture, paintings and family photographs.

MOLENMUSEUM DE VALK;
TUE-SAT 10-7, SUN 1-5
www.molenmuseumdevalk.nl

2 Leave the windmill and leave the park by the south exit. Cross Binnenvestgracht and walk down the left side of Nieuwe Beestenmarkt for about 200yd (183m), to Oude Singel, a narrow canal. Ahead of you is Turfmarkt. To your right is Beestenmarkt, originally Leiden's livestock market but now a dull utilitarian square surrounded by mainly modern buildings. Turn left on Oude Singel, with the canal on your right, and walk one very short block to turn left into the Stedelijk Museum de Lakenhal at Oude Singel 32 (the entrance is via the museum's modern wing).

The Lakenhal was the city's Cloth Hall and the seat of the powerful Clothier's Guild. Built in 1640, its classical portico and pediment were clearly designed to show off the guild's wealth; a stone carving of a windmill crowns the portico. As well as grinding grain and pumping water, wind power was integral to the cloth industry. On the ground floor are paintings by Rembrandt's teacher Jacob van Swanenburg, Rembrandt himself (represented here by only a handful of minor works), and his contemporary Jan Lievens. Most interesting are the

OPPOSITE: INTERIOR OF STUDY ROOM, MOLENMUSEUM DE VALK

DISTANCE **4 miles (6.4km)**

ALLOW **2.5 hours**

START **Leiden Station**

FINISH **Leiden Station**

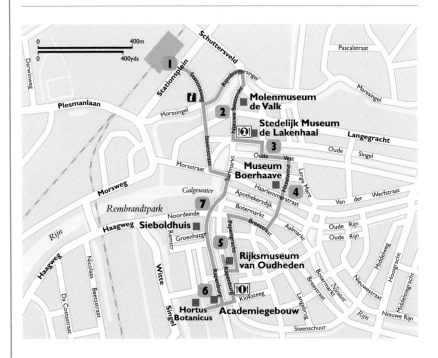

charming little paintings, crammed with detail, by Gerrit Dou (1613–75), Rembrandt's first disciple, who went on to create a style of his own which was later followed by other Leiden painters.

STEDELIJK MUSEUM DE LAKENHAL;
TUE-FRI 10-5, SUN 12-5 www.lakenhal.nl

3 Turn left out of the museum, then almost immediately right to cross the Oude Singel to Oude Vest on the opposite bank. Now turn left and walk for one short block, and take the next

right into narrow Hazewindsteeg. Follow the righthand side of this for one short block (the Leydens Schouwburg theatre is on your right for the first block); continue along Hazewindsteeg for one block, then turn right onto Lange St Agnietenstraat, and after one short block turn right into the Museum Boerhaave at Lange St Agnietenstraat 10.

The high point of this museum is the exact copy of an 18th-century anatomical theatre, with tiers of wooden seats that

WHERE TO EAT

🍴 BARRERA,
Rapenburg 56;
Tel: 071 514 6631.
www.cafebarrera.nl
Facing the Hortus Botanicus, this lively café bar has a huge drinks menu and serves a range of tapas and other snacks. Tables outdoors in summer. €

🍴 WATERLIJN CAFÉ,
Prinssessekade 2;
Tel: 071 512 1279.
www.kroegpagina.nl/waterlijn
On a pontoon moored on the right bank of the Oude Singel, this café has a great location. €

allowed medical students a clear view of the corpse being dissected by their professor. A collection of grinning skeletons stands guard, so it's all rather grisly. The museum is named after distinguished anatomist, surgeon, botanist and chemist, Hermann Boerhaave (1668-1738), a leading light of Leiden University's medical faculty.

It also celebrates other famed Leiden scientists, including Antonij van Leeuwenhoek (1632-1723), whose invention of the microscope and discovery of micro-organisms eventually revolutionized medical science, and Christian Huygens (1629-93), clockmaker, perfecter of the pendulum clock, and astronomer. Huygens also improved the telescope, enabling him to discover Titan, the largest moon of the planet Saturn. In 2005 the European Space Agency landed a spacecraft named after him on its surface.

The self-taught van Leeuwenhoek's brilliance in lens making was the key to his discoveries, which in 1680 earned him membership in England's newly founded Royal Society, created by Charles II to foster scientific brilliance. Some of his microscopes, and Huygens's telescopes and clocks, are among the museum's collection on the upper floor.

4 Double back to Hazewindsteeg; turn right and follow it as it curves right for one block to Haarlemmerstraat. Turn left, then immediately right across the Vrouwensteeg bridge and cross Aalmarkt (as its name implies, this was the old eel market – eels from the canals were a staple of the Dutch diet). Carry on for one short block to Breestraat (the Stadsgehoorzal theatre should be on your left at the corner); cross Breestraat and turn right. Pass Pieterskerkstraat on your left, then Schoolsteg, and take the third left, Papengracht. Continue for two short blocks, crossing Langebrug, to Houtstraat. Turn right here, then right again at the next corner, onto Rapenburg, and turn right just after the corner to enter the Rijksmuseum van Oudheden at Rapenburg 28.

The Rijksmuseum van Oudheden (National Museum of Antiquities) has its roots in the Egyptian studies and excavations carried out by Dutch archaeologists in the 19th and 20th centuries. A small Roman-Egyptian building, the Temple of Taffeh, dominates the ground floor. It was donated by the Egyptian government in thanks for the Dutch contribution to saving the antiquities of Abu Simbel and other sites from flooding, following the building of the Aswan Dam in the 1960s. A collection to gladden the heart of Indiana Jones is arrayed on the ground floor and includes dozens of mummies, sarcophagi and Greek and Roman relics. The upper floor is dedicated to archaeological finds from the Netherlands.

RIJKSMUSEUM VAN OUDHEDEN;

TUE-FRI 10-5 SAT-SUN 12-5 www.rmo.nl

5 Exit the museum and turn left along Rapenburg for one block to the Kloksteeg bridge, which you can see in front of you. Turn right here to cross the canal and cross to the landward side of Rapenburg. On the corner, at No. 73, is the Academiegebouw, the venerable senate building of Leiden University, built in 1581, and the Hortus Botanicus. The garden is divided into several sections. Enter, pass through the courtyard garden, and then turn left to walk to the Clusius Garden.

The Netherlands owes both the tulip and the potato to Carolus Clusius, the father of modern botany. Born Charles de l'Ecluse near Antwerp in 1526, he studied law and medicine – a science that then overlapped with the study of medicinal plants – before becoming medicinal gardener to Maximilian II, the Holy Roman Emperor, in Vienna. Maximilian's

successor, Rudolf II, sacked him, and he came to Leiden at the age of 67 to set up the university's botanical garden, and is credited with first introducing the tulip (from Asia Minor) and the spud (from America) to Dutch gardens.

6 Stroll clockwise round the gardens then leave the way you came in. Turn left to walk north along the west side of Rapenburg, with the canal on your right for two blocks, crossing Doelensteeg and Groenhazengracht on your left. Just after crossing Groenhazengracht, turn left to enter the SieboldHuis at Rapenburg 19.

The Dutch connection with Japan is easily forgotten, but the Dutch were among the first Europeans to visit Japan, setting up a trading colony in Nagasaki in 1609. The Bavarian doctor Philipp Franz von Siebold visited Japan in 1826, and his collection of works of art, stuffed birds and beasts, maps and fossils, forms the core of this fascinating collection, housed in a canal-facing three-storey mansion.

SIEBOLDHUIS;

TUE-SUN 10-5 www.sieboldhuis.org

7 Leaving the Sieboldhuis, turn left and continue north to the end of Rapenburg. Continue on Kort Rapenburg, then Prinsessekade, crossing the Galgewater canal. At the corner of Prinsessekade and Haarlemmerstraat, turn left across the Oude Singel bridge. Turn right on Steenstraat, and follow this across the Morssingel bridge to return to Stationsweg and Leiden station.

DE VALK WINDMILL WITH BEESTENMARKT IN THE FOREGROUND

INDEX

175

ACKNOWLEDGEMENTS

The Automobile Association would like to thank the following photographers, companies and picture libraries for their assistance in the preparation of this book.

Abbreviations for the picture credits are as follows – (AA) AA World Travel Library.

Front cover: Jon Hicks/Corbis; 3 Getty Images/Karen Desjardin; 7 Jon Hicks/Corbis; 8–11 World Pictures/ Photoshot; 12-13 Atlantide Phototravel/Corbis; 14 Getty Images/Frans Lemmens; 17 Christian Sarramon/Corbis; 19 Private Collection/The Bridgeman Art Library; 20-21 Lonely Planet Images/Martin Moos; 22 Amsterdam Tourism & Convention Board; 25 Barry Lewis/Corbis; 27 eye35.com/Alamy; 28 Richard T. Nowitz/Corbis; 30 World Pictures/Photoshot; 33 Art Kowalsky/Alamy; 34 Barry Lewis/Alamy; 36 travelstock44/Alamy; 39 Visual&Written SL/Alamy; 40 Sylvia Cordaiy Photo Library Ltd/Alamy; 42 Yadid Levy/Alamy; 45 World Pictures/ Photoshot; 46 Arco Images GmbH/Alamy; 48-49 Nathan Benn/Alamy; 50 World Pictures/Photoshot; 53 Bildarchiv Monheim GmbH/Alamy; 56 Art Kowalsky/Alamy; 57 The Print Collector/Alamy; 59 Jon Arnold Images Ltd/ Alamy; 60-61 John Van Hasselt/Corbis Sygma; 62 Louise Heusinkveld/Alamy; 65 Iain Masterton/Alamy; 66 World Pictures/Photoshot; 68-69 jaxpix/Alamy; 70 Jochen Tack/Alamy; 71 Richard Wareham Fotografie/Alamy; 73-74 Ingolf Pompe 2/Alamy; 76-77 Alberto Paredes/Alamy; 78 Westend61/Alamy; 81 Barry Lewis/Alamy; 84-85 Stefano Paterna/Alamy; 86 Jon Hicks/Corbis; 90-91 World Pictures/Photoshot; 92 Arco Images GmbH/Alamy; 93 Andrew Woodley/Alamy; 95 image france/Alamy; 97 Richard Wareham Fotografie/Alamy; 98-99 Amsterdam Tourism & Convention Board; 101 Amsterdam Tourism & Convention Board ; 103-104 Amsterdam Tourism & Convention Board; 106 Ken Welsh/Alamy; 109 Peter Horree/Alamy; 110 Arcaid/Alamy; 112-113 Jochen Tack/Alamy; 114 Terry Smith Images/Alamy; 118 The Smallest Gallery; 119 The Rock Archive; 120 Electric Ladyland Museum; 123 Houseboat Museum; 125 TassenMuseum; 126-127 Houseboat Museum; 128 Boerderij Meerzicht; 132 Free Agents Limited/Corbis; 135 Robert Harding Picture Library Ltd/Alamy; 136 Amsterdam Tourism & Convention Board; 138 Tony Arruza/Corbis; 141 Dave Bartruff/Corbis; 142 Sherab/Alamy; 144-145 wim wiskerke/Alamy; 146 Lee Foster/ Alamy; 150-151 Frans Hals Museum, Haarlem /The Bridgeman Art Library; 152 E. Teister/Still Pictures; 155 Wilmar Photography/Alamy; 156 Peter Horree/Alamy; 158-159 Tack/Still Pictures; 160 Michael John Kielty/Corbis; 164-165 Dave Bartruff/Corbis; 166-169 Fons Vrouenraths/Alamy; 172-173 Jon Hicks/Corbis.

Every effort has been made to trace the copyright holders, and we apologize in advance for any accidental errors. We would be happy to apply the corrections in the following edition of this publication.